'If you are serious about leaving a legacy for your school, you must ensure it is fit for the future. *FutureSchool* inspires school leaders to make the very hard and important decisions that are needed, though exploring already successful blueprints that can be adopted and adapted to create solid foundations, and build the schools our children deserve.'

Gwyn ap Hari, *Founder and CEO of the XP Schools, United Kingdom*

'Forget Deschooling. Embrace Reschooling. *FutureSchool* is a thoroughly compelling and convincing account of the power of redesigned schools to transform learning – to build our capacity to create a thriving future for all. Read it. Be uplifted.'

Anthony Mackay AM, *CEO and Board Co-Chair of the National Center on Education and the Economy, USA, and Co-Chair of Learning Creates, Australia*

'We tend to imagine school as buildings, but Valerie Hannon shows us the values and design principles that bring together the people, the spaces and the technology in new ways to educate learners for their future, rather than our past. What makes the book special are numerous case studies that reveal this future is already here, and that point us to ways how it can take root in our education systems.'

Andreas Schleicher, *Director for Education and Skills and Special Advisor on Education Policy to the Secretary-General at the Organisation for Economic Co-operation and Development (OECD)*

'If you want a school where students learn to care for themselves, others and the planet while preparing for an unpredictable future this book is for you. You will learn how schools across the world inspire and empower learners to contribute to face the challenges of our time and how this could be done in your very school.'

Professor Francois Taddei, *UNESCO USPC Chair in Learning sciences and Founder and Chair of the Centre for Research and Interdisciplinarity, University of Paris*

FutureSchool

What will the schools of the future look like? What will guide their design, and what is happening now to create them? As we enter the age of disruption and hyperchange, it has become increasingly clear that our education systems are not adequate to the task of enabling young people to thrive in a very different future.

FutureSchool offers system leaders, principals, and teachers research-based design principles upon which the evolution of schools might be based. Shaped by an awareness of changing economies, technology, and the climate emergency, it suggests specific ways that leaders can address the challenges of moving forward, grasping the opportunities presented by the disruption of the COVID-19 pandemic. Presenting six 'archetypes for the future' – key missions that are central to the future of humanity – it offers inspiring examples of practice that are not just theoretical but well-advanced in schools across the world, practice that is grounded in principles that are central to a new learning paradigm.

This book offers an answer and presents a vision that is engaging, inspiring, and intent on enabling success for all learners. This book will provide inspiration and practical guidance for leaders, teachers, and parents who want to see schools rapidly evolve to become the institutions we really need.

Valerie Hannon is a global thought leader, inspiring systems to re-think what 'success' will mean in the twenty-first century and the implications for education. Valerie is a radical voice for change, whilst grounded in a deep understanding of how education systems currently work. A former Director of Education, she has been an adviser to the UK Department of Education and to the OECD.

Julie Temperley is a researcher working to improve outcomes in education and children's social care. She is Senior Associate at Innovation Unit and several education charities.

FutureSchool

How Schools Around the World are
Applying Learning Design Principles
For a New Era

Valerie Hannon with Julie Temperley

LONDON AND NEW YORK

Cover image: © Getty Images

First published 2022
by Routledge
4 Park Square, Milton Park, Abingdon, Oxon OX14 4RN

and by Routledge
605 Third Avenue, New York, NY 10158

Routledge is an imprint of the Taylor & Francis Group, an informa business

© 2022 Valerie Hannon, Julie Temperley

The right of Valerie Hannon and Julie Temperley to be identified as authors of this work has been asserted in accordance with sections 77 and 78 of the Copyright, Designs and Patents Act 1988.

All rights reserved. No part of this book may be reprinted or reproduced or utilised in any form or by any electronic, mechanical, or other means, now known or hereafter invented, including photocopying and recording, or in any information storage or retrieval system, without permission in writing from the publishers.

Trademark notice: Product or corporate names may be trademarks or registered trademarks, and are used only for identification and explanation without intent to infringe.

British Library Cataloguing-in-Publication Data
A catalogue record for this book is available from the British Library

Library of Congress Cataloging-in-Publication Data
Names: Hannon, Valerie, author. | Temperley, Julie, author.
Title: Futureschool : how schools around the world are applying learning design principles for a new era / Valerie Hannon, with Julie Temperley.
Other titles: Future school
Description: First Edition. | New York : Routledge, 2022. | Includes bibliographical references and index. | Contents: Foreword / by Ellen Koshland, Founder The Australian Learning Lecture -- Six Schools for the Future? -- The Pandemic Shock: Enter The Future -- Design Principles from Futures Thinking -- Design Principles in Action: Values -- Design Principles in Action: Operational Philosophies -- Design Principles in Action: Learner Experience -- Can Schools Save Us? Emerging Archetypes -- The Leadership Challenge of a Generation. | Identifiers: LCCN 2021056478 (print) | LCCN 2021056479 (ebook) | ISBN 9781032154398 (Hardback) | ISBN 9781032154428 (Paperback) | ISBN 9781003244172 (eBook)
Subjects: LCSH: Educational change. | Educational innovations. | Educational leadership. | Education and globalization. | Education and state. | Critical pedagogy.
Classification: LCC LB2806 .H336 2022 (print) | LCC LB2806 (ebook) | DDC 370--dc23/eng/20220310
LC record available at https://lccn.loc.gov/2021056478
LC ebook record available at https://lccn.loc.gov/2021056479

ISBN: 978-1-032-15439-8 (hbk)
ISBN: 978-1-032-15442-8 (pbk)
ISBN: 978-1-003-24417-2 (ebk)

DOI: 10.4324/9781003244172

Typeset in Bembo
by Taylor & Francis Books

We dedicate this book to the descendants.
May we have been good ancestors.

Contents

List of illustrations	x
Foreword	xii
Preface	xiv
Acknowledgements	xvi

1	Six schools for the future?	1
2	The pandemic shock: enter The Future	11
3	Design principles from futures thinking	21
4	Design principles in action: Values	35
5	Design principles in action: Operational philosophy	46
6	Design principles in action: Learner experience	56
7	Can schools save us? Emerging archetypes	68
8	The leadership challenge of a generation	78

Appendix	93
Index	94

Illustrations

Figures

1.1 A LearnLife week	7
1.2 This book's journey	10
2.1 Step two	14
2.2 The Futures Cone	15
3.1 Step three	23
3.2 OECD future landscape	28
3.3 Step four	29
3.4 Clusters of design principles	30
3.5 Design principles on values	31
3.6 Design principles on operational philosophy	32
3.7 Design principles on learner experience	33
4.1 Step 5	35
4.2 Design principles – values	35
5.1 Design principles – operational philosophy	47
6.1 Design principles – learner experience	57
7.1 Step six	68
7.2 Six archetypes for the future?	69
7.3 Four levels of thriving	74
8.1 Three-horizon thinking	88

Boxes

Knowledge Works	25
OECD programs: Innovative Learning Environments and Framework for Education and Skills 2030	26
The First People's Principles of Learning	28
Design principle 1: Purpose driven	36
Design principle 2: Equity-focused	38
Design principle 3: Promoting identity	39
Design principle 4: Strength-based	41
Design principle 5: Relevant	42

List of illustrations xi

Design principle 6: Learning focused	46
Design principle 7: Flexible/dynamic	49
Design principle 8: Technology enhanced	50
Design principle 9: Ecosystemic	52
Design principle 10: Personalised	56
Design principle 11: Integrated	59
Design principle 12: Inclusive	60
Design principle 13: Relational	61
Design principle 14: Empowering	63
Scenario one: Schooling extended	89
Scenario two: Education outsourced	89
Scenario three: Schools as Learning Hubs	89
Scenario four: Learn-as-you-go	90

Foreword

The Australian Learning Lecture (ALL) exists to bring big ideas in education to public attention. And there is no bigger idea than *The FutureSchool*.

Therefore, it is a great pleasure to introduce this book and to have contributed to its development.

Before COVID struck the world in March 2020, Valerie Hannon was poised to deliver the third Australian Learning Lecture on *The FutureSchool* in Melbourne and Sydney. Valerie is an outstanding thought leader who has worked with many countries around the world to transform schooling.

The FutureSchool was ALL's chosen topic because people around us were asking what would significant change in schooling look like to meet the needs of the future? Many people had understood that students needed new skill sets — but how exactly would that translate into new models of schools?

We were thrilled that Valerie accepted our invitation to conduct a global scan and analysis of the nature of the future school. The deep thinking that she and Julie Temperley undertook over the year before COVID was shaped by the idea that *seeing is believing*.

And it has stood a major test of time. Not only does the case still hold up; in a world where disruption is normalised, it has become more compelling.

Valerie presents a cohesive view of a way forward for education. She identified more than 50 future schools already operating — and there could have been many more. While different circumstances in schools around the world are celebrated, her research identified a core set of principles that guides them all.

I believe we owe it to our young people today to prepare and enable every one of them for the future ahead. They deserve to look forward with confidence and with positive, strong foundations.

Schools are core to the well-being of society. In a world of enduring disruption, the imperative to make them centres of exciting, purposeful learning is greater than ever.

We hope the ideas and schools profiled in this book inspire your thoughts and shared discussion. And, more than that, that they help inspire and chart a journey to new effective practice.

Ellen Koshland
Founder, Australian Learning Lecture

Preface

If there was ever a moment when the role and value of the institution of 'school' came under the spotlight, it was the year 2020.

There were very few silver linings to the tragic occurrence of COVID-19, but it did lead to a greater public awareness of some of the issues that had preoccupied those calling for a paradigm shift in education.

Those calls arose from the perception that humanity is at a pivotal point in its history. Opportunities sit beside great threats. The actions that we (and particularly the young) take in the coming decades will be critical. It is as fallacious to resign to an apocalyptic future as it is to pretend that the future will be like the past. But we should recognise a change in the zeitgeist. There is now a widespread sense of dread about the future. Where once there was optimism, many young people seem drenched in pessimism.

This book arises out of the opportunity offered to the principal author to deliver the 2020 Australian Learning Lecture, with the title *The FutureSchool*. A week before it was due to take place, COVID-19 struck. Though the event did not happen, the research had been completed and in the months that followed, the theme of the lecture was suddenly one of intense interest; since 'school' as we knew it was interrupted, the question everywhere was asked: should schools revert to 'normal'? And if not, what might guide the changes to be made? What might a new model look like – in practice, not just in theory?

This book explores that question – not from an idealistic or theoretical standpoint – but empirically. We examine how innovators across the world have already been intentionally redesigning schools for the future.

The empirical foundation comprises, first, a database of future-focused organisations – from intergovernmental research agencies, to challenge-prize sponsors to think-tanks. The work of these organisations was examined, revealing a set of *design principles* for future schools. A large dataset of schools instantiating these principles was then assembled. It is the work of these schools that lies at the heart of this book.

We look at future-focused schools in diverse settings – from California to Delhi, from New Zealand to Spain – to explore the thinking that has led to their establishment, the practical new models that have resulted, and consider what they might have to teach us about what a new 'normal' might look like; one that is focused on creating the future the next generation needs.

We end the book with a discussion of the implications of all this for leaders: political, system, institutional, and community leaders, all of whom have a critical role to play in propelling us towards public arrangements for learning that are up to the job of creating the future we want. "Propelling" because it is urgent. Of course, parents and learners themselves have a huge role to play in all of this, and the efforts around the world in co-creation and co-design are modelling that. But we focus here on what leaders need to do, to utilise the learnings arising from the 2020 pandemic, and all the work profiled here, to create a new public discourse and sets of possibilities. That new narrative needs to inspire imagination and innovation, which will be decisive in transforming what is possible into a desired reality.

Acknowledgements

Many people have contributed to this volume over a few years, through their collegial sharing of ideas and intellectual generosity. First and foremost, we must thank Ellen Koshland, the founder of the Australian Learning Lecture, whose vision and creativity allowed this work to come about. Thanks too, to her great team and wonderful companions: Kathe Kirby, Andrew Hiskens, and Penny Underwood. In particular, we would like to thank: Tom Beresford, who did much of the early research work, and contributed significantly to the conceptualisation. Other generous colleagues read and commented on early drafts, and we are thankful for their critical and encouraging contributions, in particular: Louise Stoll, Michael Stevenson, Tony Mackay, Lorna Earl. Our greatest thanks are due to the school leaders who consented to be interviewed about their work and shaped our thinking. Thanks to our editor at Routledge, Vilija Stephens, for believing in the work; and to the whole Routledge team for supporting us throughout.

1 Six schools for the future?

What images come to mind when you are asked to imagine a school of the future?

Perhaps shiny 'futuristic' buildings full of technology, children with cool headsets or implants; screens, virtual reality kit, augmented reality, digital simulations, AI-driven individualised programs …

That vision may well become part of the reality. In this book we argue that the technological possibilities are but one part of the picture. However, more important by far than the application of those technologies is the job we need and want schools to do: how they are to play a part in constructing a future in which humans can truly thrive. Already across the world, educators have started to prototype such schools. In this chapter, we are going to explore that work. In doing so, we will also be building a case that schools are desperately *needed* to address the profound challenges (as well as the opportunities) we face – but only if they are fundamentally redesigned.

Schools redesigned 1: Green School, Bali

In 2016 Ruby Bourke left her home in Australia to attend the Green School in Bali. She was 15. She and her parents wanted an empowering educational experience for her that equipped her to engage effectively with perhaps the most important issue facing our future: the climate emergency.

> *I came to Green School because I aligned with the 'bigger picture' solution the school strives to achieve: progressive, sustainability-oriented. Basically, I joined a community of learners – teachers, parents, global changemakers, students all contributing equally to each other's growth and expansion of knowledge. I felt heard and acknowledged as a unique learner. At Green School, youth voice matters in conversations about our learning and about the future.*

Green School opened in 2009, on a mission. Parents, teachers, leaders and students share a single clear and explicit purpose; to grow a generation of global green leaders and citizens committed to taking better care of our planet. New campuses have recently opened in New Zealand and Mexico, with some delays to expansion plans because of COVID-19. The school educates for

DOI: 10.4324/9781003244172-1

2 Six schools for the future?

sustainability, through community-integrated, entrepreneurial learning. They believe that future generations need a wider set of tools to equip learners for an unknown new world and provide them with an understanding of sustainable living practices.

John and Cynthia Hardy are the founders. John had a Canadian childhood spent struggling through his own education with undiagnosed dyslexia: so the last thing he expected to ever do was open a school. With his wife he opened a jewellery business in Bali, a place they came to love.

The determination to create Green School grew out of watching Al Gore's *An Inconvenient Truth*, the film Hardy says that "ruined my life". Like millions of others, he was profoundly moved and challenged by what he learned about the climate emergency and its existential threat to humanity. Unlike millions of others, he decided to act.

It is impossible to overstate the significance of the physical features of the school in understanding its purpose and ethos. Built almost entirely from fast growing and therefore sustainable bamboo the school seems to grow out of the surrounding gardens, which themselves emerge from the forest where the bamboo continues to grow.

There are no walls, internal or external, creating flexible spaces for learning, which open out onto views across the gardens and into the forest, making the natural world a very real and vital presence in the learning environment. Green School is now proudly self-sufficient in solar and hydro energy, a result of a partnership with a green power company. Water is drawn from an underground source and plant-based meals are cooked on sawdust-fired ovens by local families from ingredients largely grown in the school's gardens by the staff and students.

The school serves c.520 early years, middle and high school students aged 3 to 18.

Although it is an international school, Green School is unequivocally also Balinese; it is of its place. One fifth of students are Balinese and pay no fees. Almost 100% of students proceed to college. All students learn about Indonesian history and culture and practice traditional crafts with local artisans; it is a part of the local ecosystem.

The curriculum integrates subjects and skills to more accurately reflect how things work in the real world, and is taught in six-week modules that introduce all students to an expansive range of ideas and learning opportunities. Students learn English and Maths in discrete lessons characterised by high quality teaching.

There is a structure to the day: the first two hours are given over to "discovering the world with all your senses" when students work in the garden or take part in creative and cultural activities. This is based on the premise that you do not fight for what you do not love. At lunchtime the whole school community eats together and there is a mindfulness pause before learning resumes.

When the COVID-19 pandemic struck in early 2020, staff at Green School pivoted swiftly to deal with its consequences, creating the *Green School Everywhere* learning portal to enable learning and teaching to continue, to stay

Six schools for the future?   3

connected, to recruit parents as teachers (for all, not just their own) and learners as teachers too. The graduating capstone project presentations (*The Greenstone* for Gr 12 and *The Quest* for Gr 8) were recorded and broadcast to far greater numbers than could previously be present.

Sal Gordon, Principal of the school, feels that the crisis was seized as an opportunity to extend reach, and add a new set of pedagogic methods to the school's repertoire, using digital tools for asynchronous learning. Still, for him, the relational dimension uniquely enabled by physical presence is irreplaceable:

> *Relationship building is so key: with each other and with the environment itself. That's at the heart of how we build values here, and the confidence in our learners that they can be changemakers on behalf of the planet. But after the challenges of COVID-19 we will be going forward to school, not back to school[1].*

Ruby Bourke, post-COVID, is to become a campaigner for a climate justice charity, based in Tasmania.

Schools redesigned 2: **Liger Leadership Academy, Cambodia**

Liger Leadership Academy (LLA) is based in Phnom Penh, Cambodia. It educates promising youth – in a historical context of profound trauma – to become socially conscious, entrepreneurial leaders of tomorrow. The school provides a residential scholarship program for economically disadvantaged students that combines a comprehensive, internationally competitive education with an innovative STEM and entrepreneurship curriculum.

Liger's model is highly empowering: it has enabled young leaders to excel beyond traditional subjects. Liger students have become internationally published authors, app and digital currency developers, regionally recognised robotics engineers, and national award-winning filmmakers – all by the age of 15. Teachers are called facilitators because they work alongside students to identify a problem or opportunity and design solutions, ideas and products to address that problem.

LLA seeks to integrate learning. The program comprises explorations, essentials, expertise and advanced enrichment. EXPLORATIONS are Liger's project-based learning experiences focused on finding solutions to real-world problems. ESSENTIALS are their core classes in English literacy, Khmer literacy, math and science. The EXPERTISE element comprises learning experiences available to LLA's senior cohort that allow students to gain a deeper knowledge or expertise in areas of interest or excellence. ADVANCED ENRICHMENTS are learning experiences available to LLA's junior cohort that help students to develop an understanding of the world around them and provide a frame of reference for future long-term projects.

EXPLORATIONS at LLA are project-based experiences where students work together in groups of 12 to explore a relevant, often complex question, problem or challenge. This project-based learning is almost always enhanced

4 *Six schools for the future?*

with intensive activities that involve student immersion in real-world experiences outside of the classroom.

Jeff Holte is the Director of Education for LLA. He is a passionate exponent of the power of purpose; and of creating a learning ecosystem:

> *We take very seriously our goals. What is a good leader? A combination of what we call leadership competencies: vision and influencing; networking and problem-solving; communication and joining the dots. But also their whole value system: integrity and honesty; do they **care**? This is the basis for our whole curriculum that we think will take them into the future and create a better country. For the first time in my career I have seen what it looks like when students are totally engaged in their learning.*
>
> *Our real-world projects – for example, reviving the coastline of Cambodia – have forced us to ask: who is a teacher? When you realise that the whole world has opened up, and the world is a classroom, then the answer can be – everyone. Because teachers just can't know everything.*

Schools redesigned 3: Kosen Schools, Japan

The Kosen Schools in Japan have set out to find a meaningful way to prepare students not just for the digitally automated workplace, but also to develop the entrepreneurial and problem-solving competencies to shape the technologies of the future towards humanistic and planetary flourishing.

Today (and even more so in the future) to achieve excellence in future-focused technologies as an unconnected school is a near impossibility. As of 2021, there were 57 Kosen across Japan, including 51 National Institutes of Technology – with a small number of private and offshore Kosen being built both in Japan and countries like Thailand, Vietnam and Mongolia.

All Kosen (National Colleges of Technology) have Collaborative Technology Centres in order to enhance their educational and research functions and stimulate the regional economy. The centres deal with collaborative research with private companies, technical support and so on. Thus, the schools are powerfully networked; ecosystemic in their approach. There is very close cooperation with industry: a long-term internship (over a month) is required and engineers from industry complement the faculty.

Students can enrol in the five-year engineering programme at the age of 15. Upon successful completion, students graduate with the equivalent of an associate degree. Following this, students can choose to attend a two-year advanced course and graduate with the equivalent of a bachelor's degree. Kosens provide a highly specialised and fast-tracked five-year curriculum to expedite the training process that would normally take at least seven years to achieve through ordinary senior high schools and bachelor's degrees. In the unique labour market of Japan – with strong manufacturing and innovation sectors, on-the-job training tradition and preference for younger graduates – Kosen graduates continue to be attractive to companies.

Kosen organises inter-college competitions, such as the Robot Contest, Programming Contest, and Design Contests. Naturally, the possibilities and issues around artificial intelligence (AI) are a particular focus. Kosen students are encouraged to develop a broad outlook on engineering by blending the specialties of regular course graduates who have studied in different fields. The schools also foster a sense for business, since relevance is of the utmost importance.

In 2019, the Deep Learning Contest (Dcon) was introduced, where Kosen student teams presented business plans, centred around products and services they have developed, to the panel of Venture Capital executives. The winning team from Nagaoka Kosen — made up of two international students from Mongolia and a Japanese student — created METERAI, an AI-assisted system that monitors and analyses the information from numerous *analog* metres used in factories to improve energy efficiency and product consistency. Bourbon, a famous confectionary company based in the local area, had already trialled the system and saw a 30% reduction in their electricity usage[2].

The Kosen curriculum emphasises scientific experiments, workshop training and practical manufacturing skills. Kosen students will typically work for several years on developing and realising their big ideas. Toshiki Tomihira, a student specialising in electrical engineering, developed a virtual reality experience of wild-water rafting. Daisuke Suzuki, a chemistry student, is working on a low-cost solution to purify soil from heavy metal pollution. But unlike most other school projects, the fruits of the work of Kosen students typically end up not in a bin, but in an incubator where they find their way to market as one of Japan's many innovations.

At Kosen schools, in order to realise their ambition to be learner-centred, the conventional role of teacher has evolved: here, they are mainly coaches, mentors, facilitators and evaluators.

Schools redesigned 4: **Tri-County Early College, USA**

In 2006, Tri-County Early College (TCEC), North Carolina, opened its doors to students as a part of the Clay and Cherokee County Public Schools system. It is located on the campus of its post-secondary partner, Tri-County Community College. It began as a start-up, with support from the Gates Foundation. Whilst it is a part of the public system, TCEC operates differently. From age 14, students can sit in on classes in the college: and have the opportunity to earn an Associates two-year degree. TCEC sets out to ensure its students are confident and prepared to enter the new world of work, and this is reflected in the strong emphasis on job shadowing and career development throughout these high-school years. This emphasis can be found too in Big Picture Schools[3] across the world, where internships are always an integral part of the model.

At TCEC the target population is first-generation college goers, those at risk of dropping out or other historically underserved groups. The school is scheduled to become part of a multi-purpose Career Academy to expand and diversify

6   *Six schools for the future?*

vocational opportunities to its students. Of course, TCEC is not about just one thing. It also emphasises volunteering and community service. However, the school places special emphasis on the fact that its alumni are forging successful careers around the country.

Naturally the school aims to connect students to the world beyond the classroom, emphasising relevance. Students have a non-traditional schedule, with small class sizes offering personalised learning. They focus on hands-on, project-based, integrated teaching and learning, with built-in tutoring. TCEC is an Open-Source Learning School and as an XQ Super School Finalist, intended to share its practice with schools anywhere in the world.

To create the mindset that TCEC believes is essential to navigate success in the world of work, a strengths-based approach is vital, and the school manifests this in its approach to assessment. It changed the conventional grading system to a competency-based model that is flexible enough to allow each student to master the knowledge and skills they need when they are ready. Students meet on a bi-weekly basis with their Learning Guide Adviser to ensure they are making the progress they need on their projects and their mastery of competencies. This is also a time of structured reflection, analysis, and synthesis of academic skills with TCEC's 'survival skills'.

Schools redesigned 5: **LearnLife, Barcelona**

A fateful meeting ignited the spark that led to the establishment of LearnLife, based in Catalonia, Spain. Christopher Pommerening was a venture capitalist entrepreneur, living in Barcelona. Like many informed parents, he was dismayed by the educational options available for his young family (even in the elite private sector). He began a worldwide search for a different vision of education. Stephen Harris was a highly respected Principal of a large secondary school in the north of Sydney, which he had served for 19 years. But Stephen was a restless, dissatisfied educator. He had long been researching and implementing new ideas for how learning in the future could be. Now, he was offered a blank slate to put them all together, and to evolve a model – not just for that school's students, but for other educators to learn from too.

Together Stephen and Christopher have established LearnLife: at its heart is the idea that schools need *to grow changemakers and entrepreneurs.*

LearnLife describes itself as a 'learning hub'. It has intentionally sought to assemble a new paradigm for learning, which is a practical version of aggregated and current educational research, especially with respect to cognitive neuroscience, psychology and learning. This has translated into a set of design principles that have guided the school's work.

Attention to these principles has disrupted the conventional use of space, time and people. Housed in a city-centre location, LearnLife has created a studio-style learning environment – light, attractive and interesting, with cutting edge facilities. It co-houses some small businesses as 'co-workers'; and welcomes 'co-learners', aged 18 to 20. LearnLife took COVID shutdown in its stride, morphing its programme to accommodate distance learning. It also hosted a series of online 'conversations' (then podcasts) for educators worldwide, to explore the opportunities and challenges thrown up by the pandemic shutdown.

The school itself has a capacity of 125 full-time learners, plus a further 150 (all ages) in casual – evening or weekend – programmes. Learners are grouped into

- Explorers – 11- to 14-year-olds
- Creators – 14- to 16-year-olds
- Changemakers – 16+

A primary programme is due to commence in 2020/21.

Here is a what a typical week looks like, though LearnLife aims to be agile and flexible in its scheduling:

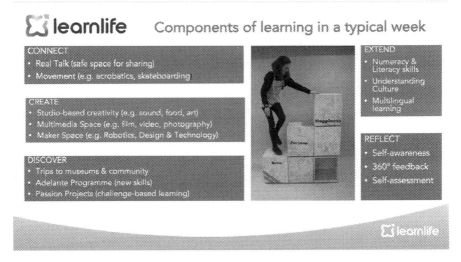

Figure 1.1 A LearnLife week

Stephen Harris says that a number of principles are completely fundamental to LearnLife's approach:

> For me there is absolutely no reason why every child should not enjoy the learning process and succeed in it. That means: what do WE have to change to meet a child's needs? Relationships are at the heart of it. Inclusivity. Respect. We are about creating independent learners. They leave with a portfolio of learning. If they want to go to university, they present a piece of research. But most of our kids want to pursue further learning pathways that take them on the road to entrepreneurship.

8   *Six schools for the future?*

Schools redesigned 6: **Nga Tapuwae, New Zealand**

Arihia Stirling is the much-honoured founding Principal of the Nga Tapuwae school in Auckland, New Zealand. (Translation: *The Footsteps of the Ancestors.*) All learners at the school are of Maori heritage, and it is Maori language immersive. Arihia believes that secure understanding of their learners' identity in the modern context is fundamental:

> *We need to ensure that our children inhabit a space where they can feel safe about their identity. Understanding who they are, where they are, where they come from – that's what improves their self-efficacy. As Maori, we come from quite a broken space. Our children need to know that they don't need to stay there: they need to under-stand how important their Maori-ness is. Their language. Their connections. If you have a nurturing cultural environment at school, then the children understand that learning resides in their identity, not in an institution[4].*

This school believes that in order to create successful futures, young people need to discover who they are, together with a sense of belonging.

Nga Tapuwae is an all-through school educating from kindergarten to year 13. The school's ethos is that students need a strong and embedded understanding of themselves as Maori, as "a proud and productive people, pre- and post-colonisation".

The school draws strongly upon the cultural assets that are available, working towards a school deeply embedded in its community and reaching beyond its own resources to leverage learning expertise and opportunities from elsewhere. An integrated curriculum is expressed in incorporating indigenous dimensions of knowledge: conservation, food gathering, hunting, fishing. It should not be assumed, though, that this is a primitive approach to curriculum: the school was an early adopter of cloud-based curriculum resources. For Arihia Stirling, an integrated curriculum incorporates values at all stages:

> *The world is asking for a different kind of human being now: someone who knows how to connect, that is truly present. You bring the best part of yourself. The world is needing us to be honest and upfront[5].*

Like many of our other future-ready schools, learners at Nga Tupuwae were well-placed to cope with the 2020 pandemic shutdown. New Zealand as a country was exceptionally wisely led through the crisis, and was the first to reopen after full shutdown. Nevertheless, schools were shut for a full seven weeks. A strong online learning offer was well used by learners who were highly independent; it led to an even greater assertiveness on their part, and a legacy of more blended learning pat-terns. Going forward, at the time of writing, the school was discussing with its Board what should be the required attendance pattern for the future, and looking for flexibility in this. Staff felt that students returned to school more reflective, kinder – and more appreciative of the school as social space. Like so many of the schools we

Six schools for the future? 9

have profiled, the pandemic experience drove social and emotional learning even further to the core of what the school is about.

However, in 2020 too, the explosion of protest, anger and frustration expressed through the *Black Lives Matter* campaign impacted all schools. With its overarching emphasis on their learners acquiring a powerful sense of identity as Maori, Nga Tapuwae had a calm, centred response to the waves of emotion and turbulence the events provoked. With its deep exploration of issues of identity for people of colour in the context of New Zealand's colonial history, Nga Tapuwae had already developed a pedagogy and curriculum (grounded in its principles) that addressed these issues head-on; with the explicit intention of bringing into the world healers of racial division and injustice from a place of pride and authentic identity. Schools that scaffold the search for identity that all young people experience will surely be a part of creating liveable futures for humans on earth.

Arihia Stirling makes the point that the search for identity is universal.

> *From a global perspective, whatever the cultural context, the identity they [learners] bring is so important. We believe in 'ancestrally driven, future-focused'. Everyone has something they can connect to in that statement.*

That is an inspirational insight right now. Obviously, in the case of racial injustice and oppression, but also in the context of migration, mixed race heritage and in some cultures, the dangerous loss of coherent narrative about identity for the white working class, especially males.

The search for FutureSchool

These six exemplar schools are surely inspiring and exciting. Later, in Chapter 7, we argue that they are more than just exemplars: they are archetypal of important movements going on in the innovation of education today. They have emerged from our journey to find schools of the future. It's important to explain how that journey was undertaken.

The process went like this:

- A school designed for, or ready for, the future must be somehow based on precepts about how the future will look: that is, on *'futures thinking'*
- So what is 'futures thinking'? How does it help?
- What organisations have been systematically undertaking futures thinking?
- The outcomes of such thinking are *design principles* for the schools of the future
- A database was compiled of schools across the world, in diverse contexts, using these design principles. We explore how these principles are working
- The principles can be combined in different ways, with different emphases: they are ingredients, not a recipe. Some schools are combining them to attack the key issues confronting humanity: they are *archetypal* – such as the schools described earlier in this chapter – of schools fit for the future.

In search of future schools

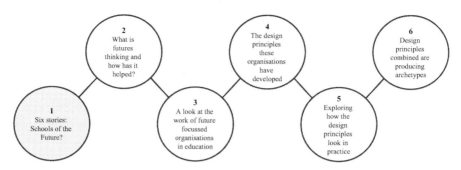

Figure 1.2 This book's journey

We begin the journey with reflections about how COVID-19 has brought futures thinking to the fore, and how a variety of organisations have deployed it.

Notes

1 Interview with author, June 2020.
2 www.businessinsider.jp/post-189980.
3 www.bigpicture.org/.
4 Interview with author, 21 October 2019.
5 Ibid.

2 The pandemic shock

Enter The Future

The virus is rewriting our imaginations. What felt impossible has become thinkable[1].

The 2020 shock

The shocking speed with which COVID-19 transformed life across the world was a wake-up call. The realisation dawned that life is not in a secure steady state. We are, like it or not, in an age of disruptions: some of them beneficial, some malign, some representing existential threat. These realisations had been vaguely on the peripheral vision of most people, but the 2020 pandemic brought it home. The experience of everyone in the world (save perhaps those living in remote tribes) was directly affected.

With it came the awareness that this is not a one-off. Aside from the likelihood of other pandemics, the prospect of the impact of the climate emergency (amongst other disruptions) started to take on a shape, as across the world, supply chains were interrupted, many millions lost their only means of support; and forcing, in some contexts, mass migrations. The concept of change at a global scale and at a rapid pace attained a reality it had previously lacked. The future just kicked the door down.

In a sense, the pandemic was like a giant X-ray machine that revealed the fissures, cracks and dark shadows in societies: not necessarily unknown, but generally disregarded. This is as true for schools and education systems as it was for other areas of life.

What did the X-ray reveal for schools?

- How enormously important the social function of schools was. On every survey about what (if anything) students missed about school the item that came top was – friends and people.
- That, notwithstanding decades of expectation that digital technology would transform learning, when it came to it, almost all schools were woefully unprepared. Technology had not been brought into the DNA of schools, and the removal of face-to-face connection revealed how primitive the majority of use was.
- That whilst some schools knew and understood their communities, it was revealed how many did not. The home circumstances and real-life conditions of their families came as a revelation to many schools.

DOI: 10.4324/9781003244172-2

12   *The pandemic shock*

- How the flexibility of *release* from mandatory attendance at school had been enjoyed by students, especially those for whom the rigidities of factory-style school routines did not fit.
- Set against this, it was revealed how the functioning of economies depended on the safe custody of children to free up parents to work. Whilst home schooling was revealed as a viable and attractive option for some (a tiny minority), most parents needed others, elsewhere, to look after their children, even as working from home became normalised.
- The fragility of the business model for much of the higher education (HE) sector. Dependency on revenues from overseas students meant that in 2020, HE institutions had to scramble to reconsider how to become viable; and the role they were to play in their home constituencies. It was revealed how they needed to refocus on their relationship with domestic learners, and the role they might play in the overall fabric of education.
- It was revealed how the standardised assessment industry consumes time, energy and money. And for what?
- Leadership is a key determinant. Whether of countries, cities or the local primary school, leadership can make the difference: between optimism and hope; vitality or despair; and in the case of the health security of nations, literally between life and death.
- The equity gap, which was already grotesque, is now unconscionable and unsustainable. Social safety nets were seen to be eroded or non-existent. Poverty and race were revealed to be preexisting conditions for vulnerability − to viral infection and many other ills. Contrasts could not be ignored in the life circumstances of children − some of whom enjoyed rich, varied and enjoyable learning experiences during lockdown; whilst others had a full stop to their learning. Some endured increased levels of domestic violence towards both women and children[2].
- The occasion of COVID-19 gave many people cause to reflect upon their values; upon what *really* mattered. Care became priceless; oil became worthless. Nature blossomed and gave solace. Relationships were understood to be at the very essence of a good life.

COVID-19 opportunity?

The pandemic caused much pain − but it also presented an immense opportunity. There were signs of this even in the midst of the turmoil schools had to contend with. Many teachers were adaptable and capable of rapidly pulling together blended programmes, and working much more closely with families. Some learners, as noted above, relished the new freedoms to plan and utilise their time. And many school leaders seized the opportunity to debate with their peers the implications for the future of what had happened.

The pandemic shock 13

This social upheaval is potentially a game changer. Policy options that previously seemed like pie-in-the-sky dreams could now move to the top of the political agenda. In some countries, the issue of the costs, benefits and value of expensive terminal exam systems became a live issue[3]. But will the opportunity be seized? Or will the tendency to 'snap back' prevail in the next decade?

After the hardships of lockdown phases there was a palpable yearning for things to return to what they had been. Up to a point. Some surveys suggested that – especially in the light of the shift in values that had occurred – there was serious appetite for change. In Canada, a large-scale survey[4] explored what Canadians wanted life to look like after the pandemic: 72% of respondents said it was an opportunity to make some major changes. In the UK, an RSA/YouGov survey found that only 9% wanted to return to what used to be called 'normal'[5].

Could this appetite be translated into a concerted and sustained programme of work to address the weaknesses in education systems, whilst building on their strengths?

As a result, the question "what could and should the future school be like?" became no longer just academic or theoretical. It became a question that now demands an answer. Suddenly, every policymaker, strategist, service provider and public servant is speculating on what the future holds for their individual areas of responsibility. It should be no different for education, though despite multiple surface changes, the basic institution of schooling has remained remarkably resilient.

Now parents are asking that question too, having in many cases had the lid taken off school cultures; and seeing the kinds of tasks their children were required to perform when in lockdown. And many learners are asking the question more insistently. Some, having tasted self-directed learning and access to high quality online resources, ask what value the school can now add.

In April 2020, the novelist and activist Arundhati Roy wrote:

> Historically, pandemics have forced humans to break with the past and imagine their world anew. This one is no different. It is a portal, a gateway between one world and the next. We can choose to walk through it, dragging the carcasses of our prejudice and hatred, our avarice, our data banks and dead ideas, our dead rivers and smoky skies behind us. Or we can walk through lightly, with little luggage, ready to imagine another world. And ready to fight for it[6].

We want systems and schools to walk through that portal, ready to imagine another world – and equipped to enable the next generation to create it

Futures thinking

In such a context, the discipline of 'futures thinking' comes into its own.

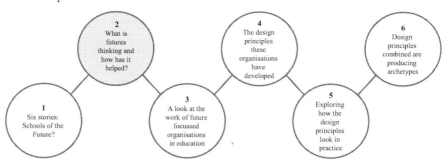

Figure 2.1 Step two

The point of futures thinking is not to get better at prediction (though that would be rather helpful). Whatever futures methodology is used, the purpose is really to stretch our imaginations by considering what is *possible*, *probable* and *preferred*.

In public policy terms *some* level of prediction is essential, as the 2020 crisis showed. The pandemic was neither unprecedented nor unpredicted. There were precedents: pandemics like the Black Death, Plague, Spanish Flu have over the centuries decimated populations, and reshaped societies[7]. Nor was the 2020 pandemic unpredicted. As an example, Bill Gates' 2015 TED talk[8] set out with some precision what was likely to happen – and indeed highly specific measures that could be taken to mitigate it. So did a number of specifically convened agencies[9]. This shows that whilst the world is an unpredictable place, unpredictability is often not the problem.

The problem is that faced with clear risks, we still fail to act. Or that in the face of a set of alternatives, choices may be left to chance rather than made intentionally. The shock of 2020 has woken people up to the need to attend to what trend data and scientific analyses are telling us about likely scenarios.

'Futures' are always constructions. They reflect the values and tools of the analysts. The difficulties of adopting 'the future' as a guide to action has been much debated by futurists[10]. In human history, we have moved from oracles, entrails and mystical prophecy through to mechanistic linear prediction to algorithms. Now though, it is argued that what is needed is futures literacy[11]. Being 'futures literate' enables people to appreciate the world more fully, to use the future to innovate the present[12].

Futures Literacy Laboratories have been supported by UNESCO across the world to help localities ask new questions and open up new horizons for innovative action[13]. And crucially, this is about enabling people to make better, wiser decisions. Rather than looking for a deterministic predictive sign, or to extrapolate from existing trends, future studies aim to evoke a much wider and deeper set of possible futures.

The possible, plausible, probable and preferred

The task of creating schools fit for the coming (and indeed present) challenges and opportunities, entails more than intoning that the "future is VUCA![14]"

Identifying the "possible, plausible, probable and preferred", we can see that this is a task both of imagination and calculation. Asking the question "what might the future school look like?" invites a narrowing scan – moving from the possible to the preferred. But it is essential that the range of the possible is wide – as in Figure 2.1 – lest we are trapped in a vision too close to what already exists.

We are used to having a relative amount of certainty in the short term. We used to know what could plausibly occur tomorrow, next month and next year, because those possibilities were often extensions of the present. But with the abrupt changes caused by COVID-19, our short-term cone of plausibility has widened significantly. We are facing a level of uncertainty we typically associate with the far-off future. We have entered the age of disruptions *experientially* – not just theoretically.

Applying futures thinking to schools and education systems

Futures thinking, as a discipline, has a history in education. The great Australian educator Hedley Beare published his important book *Creating the FutureSchool* back in 2000[15]. Much has changed since then, not all of it in the direction that Beare predicted. In general, Beare's predictions about the state of the world are about 50% right. The resulting changes he envisaged in schooling have hardly materialised.

Beare is one of a number of thinkers who have tried to focus educators' minds on possible futures[16]. But until recently, there have not been that many who have sought to bring the disciplines of futures literacy to the task.

The *OECD* deserves special mention in this context. From 2001, it has been specifically alerting systems to the disconnect between prevailing models of schooling and emergent futures. In its first publication[17] on this theme, it identified the 'driving forces' in key economic, social, cultural and policy trends. The questions posed in that early work were: What will schools look like in the future? What big trends are the most influential in shaping education, and how might these unfold in the coming years? What policy questions

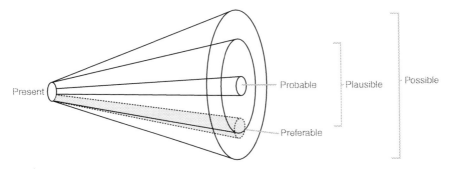

Figure 2.2 The Futures Cone

16 *The pandemic shock*

need to be tackled today for desirable pathways into the future to become more likely? The method was then to produce six scenarios (envisaged in a timescale of 10–20 years, which were grouped into three categories: 'status quo', 're-schooling' and 'de-schooling'. The work was as much concerned with the nature of systems as it was with that of institutions. This work was updated in 2020[18] and we draw upon that later in this book.

As discussed in more depth in Chapter 3, OECD has continued to explore these themes: its current work programme (2015–) looking to a 2030 horizon[19], builds upon its decades-long effort, refocusing in particular on issues of purpose. It is encouraging to observe that this work has moved much more centre stage in the interests of many OECD member countries in recent years.

In a sense, the *UN Sustainable Development Goals*[20] should be mentioned in this context since its work in seeking to unify global efforts to create desirable futures was founded on analysing future trends in the fields of poverty, inequality, climate change, environmental degradation, peace and justice. In education its approach is very broad brush, referring in general terms to 'quality' education without in-depth exploration of what that in the future will entail.

Time to write schools off?

Most of the scenario building that futures thinking has undertaken contains at least one in which the school no longer survives as an institution. Like other institutions that faded from the centre to the periphery of people's everyday preoccupations (such as the family farm or certain religious and military organisations) perhaps, post COVID-19, schools – like the 'office' – might also move off centre stage?

The prospect that schools (and further and higher education institutions) would fade away as their functions were assumed by digital modes has been repeatedly raised. Whilst hardly a new prospect – both Illych's seminal *Deschooling Society* and Reimers' *School is Dead* were published in 1971[21] – the development of the digital educational technology industry into a multi-trillion dollar prospect has really only got underway in the first decade of the 21st century.[22] Until recently it was regularly remarked that edtech (educational technology) had over-promised and under-delivered. Little evidence was found of its transformational effects on learning, nor of its capacity to displace schooling[23].

Then COVID-19 struck. It is reasonable to ask: was this the extinction event of the institutions? There are reasons to think this is a possibility. The 2020 shock of the removal of the supervisory aspects of schooling might yet give rise to more extensive experiments that do not revolve around a legally mandated:

- containment of a fixed number of students within a single set of physical boundaries, and
- pre-specified portion of the day and week.

The 'reveals' of the pandemic, set out in the opening to this chapter, could propel some systems down this path. Indeed, in the case of the global south specifically, rapid educational progress may *depend* upon not trying to replicate this model but to leapfrog it.[24]

However, before embracing this as a preferred future too hastily, we might also reflect upon a fuller set of pandemic 'reveals', emerging as the lockdowns progressed, some of which drive towards a different conclusion. Some are practical; others more profound.

The supervisory, or 'custodial' function, rather than being consigned to redundancy was actually understood to be critical. Even with parents working from home for significant portions of the week – likely to be an irreversible trend across many industries – the focused care of children, which is safe and nurturing, by other adults (even if their cognitive learning needs could be met by digital personalised means) is essential both to the functioning of economies and parents' own needs.

But the more profound reason to configure schools into our preferred future is not just pragmatic. We argue that schools must be retained in the mix: not as the only vehicles and modes for supporting 'becoming' in our young, but as a critical and desirable element – *if they can be redesigned*. We believe they are needed to equip new generations to shape the future in human terms.

However, it may well be that with rapid development of online learning and AI-driven personalised learning programmes, and given the accelerant that the 2020 shutdowns precipitated, the question of whether we need schools in the future at all becomes real.

It is hard to conceive that any government will adopt an altogether laissez-faire attitude towards the education of its children, since this is so intimately connected to the very nature of their states, not just their economies. The question is: what might they mandate? It is possible to imagine prescribed bodies of knowledge being learnt (and assessed) online. But we show in Chapter 3 how many other functions schools have been tasked to fulfil historically, and the 2020 pandemic did reveal how important it is for functioning economies – even reconstructed green economies – to care for children collectively to free parents up for other activities.

Does the school as a physical space need arguing for? The pandemic has cast new light on this. Possibly it was once thought that schooling could be 'virtualised'. But the unplanned global experiment in taking physical schools out of the mix did throw into relief some overlooked functions.

Dialling up schools' broader functions

Escape from the family is important for everyone, for different reasons in different contexts. For the disadvantaged, the physical space of school can be a respite and refuge; a source of safety, regular food, tech resources and expanded ambition. For the most advantaged, exposure to others beyond the family circle is a prerequisite to learning social competence.

Unless it is conceived as the narrow transmission of knowledge or skill acquisition, learning is a fundamentally social process. This is an insight as old as Aristotle, who said that humans are above all else social animals; and that vital

18 The pandemic shock

energy arises from gatherings – in public squares, theatres, sports stadiums. This insight has been deepened and developed through both research[25] and practice[26]. We diminish this dimension at our peril.

Making relationships with others outside the family is a vital dimension in becoming fully human. We know that good relationships make for good lives[27]. The school is the grounding for this: the space where one encounters others with different backgrounds and views, and where one learns not just to get along with, but to respect and care for others. And the sheer adventure (sometimes joyful, sometimes not) of encountering new people is one of life's gifts. Serendipity and chance in the physical world are a blessing.

Our bodies are not just vehicles for moving our brains around. The very essence of sport, of dance, of theatre, of performance, of creative arts and exhibition is *physicality*. And – even in these days of #*MeToo* heightened awareness, touch is precious. Walking arm-in-arm with a friend; a hug in tough times.

Then there is the community dimension. As social spaces, like the high street, diminish and morph, schools could become the site of various community-oriented services and facilities. In the face of social fragmentation and diversity, and the decline of various other traditional institutions playing a similar role, schools could help generate local 'social capital'. Indeed, in the schools we profile later that incorporate this work, it becomes a key dimension in citizenship learning. It is also the ground where more vibrant forms of democracy might take root. And in an age of 'democratic disappointment'[28], where the guard rails of democracy are under acute pressure from populists, coming together in micro-community will provide the spaces to explore the real meanings of democratic ideals: experientially, not just theoretically. We align ourselves with those thinkers[29] who, despite developing serious critiques of schooling in its current form, nevertheless believe that "*public institutions are the defining features of a caring and democratic society*".[30]

Let's reconstruct

So our starting point for this book is that in the future, the concept of 'school' is truly needed and relevant – but the concept is fluid and under reconstruction.

We presuppose neither stand-alone institutions, nor current attendance patterns. The utilisation of time, space, people, technology and partnerships is all open to reconsideration. But what is to guide the direction of shift? The idea of 'school' needs a new value proposition. We concur with UNESCO's conclusion:

> *We must protect the social spaces provided by schools as we transform education. The school as a physical space is indispensable. Traditional classroom organization must give way to a variety of ways of 'doing school' but the school as a separate space-time of collective living, specific and different from other spaces of learning must be preserved*[31].

Our approach has been to research those organisations and institutions for whom this is a work in progress. The next chapter presents a review of organisations that have utilised futures thinking directly on the institution of the school. The product of their efforts is a set of design principles – it is these that can provide the coordinates for the journey ahead.

Notes

1 Kim Stanley Robinson, *The New Yorker*, May 2020. www.newyorker.com/cul ture/annals-of-inquiry/the-coronavirus-and-our-future.
2 www.unicef.org.uk/coronavirus-children-in-lockdown/.
3 In Australia, see Professor Peter Shergold's Report, *Looking to the Future*, June 2020. https://uploadstorage.blob.core.windows.net/public-assets/education-au/pathways/ Final%20report%20-%2018%20June.pdf; in the UK, see the new movement, *Rethinking Assessment*, https://rethinkingassessment.com/rethinking-assessment-home.
4 www.thestar.com/politics/political-opinion/2020/05/23/the-new-normal-canadia ns-say-they-dont-want-it-to-look-much-like-the-old-one.html.
5 www.thersa.org/about-us/media/2019/brits-see-cleaner-air-stronger-social-bonds-a nd-changing-food-habits-amid-lockdown.
6 www.ft.com/content/10d8f5e8-74eb-11ea-95fe-fcd274e920ca?shareType=nongift.
7 See Diamond, J., 2005.
8 www.ted.com/talks/bill_gates_the_next_outbreak_we_re_not_ready?language=en.
9 E.g. The Global Preparedness Monitoring Board (GPMB) published a report in October 2019 *A World at Risk* alerting governments to the imminent risk; 'Exercise Cygnus' was a 2016 pandemic planning exercise, convened in the UK. Its recommendations were ignored.
10 See Gore, 2013 and Miller, 2019.
11 Miller, 2019.
12 Miller, 2011.
13 *Futures Literacy: a skill for the C21st.* UNESCO, 2020. See https://en.unesco.org/ futuresliteracy/about.
14 Volatile, Uncertain, Complex and Ambiguous. A term coined by the US military in 1987.
15 Beare, 2000.
16 Caldwell, 1998; Facer, 2011.
17 OECD, 2001.
18 OECD, 2020.
19 OECD, 2018.
20 www.un.org/sustainabledevelopment/sustainable-development-goals/.
21 Illych, 1970; Reimers, 1971.
22 In 2008, George Siemens, Stephen Downes and Dave Cormier in Canada were using web technology to create the first 'connectivist' Massive Open Online Course (MOOC).
23 Fullan, 2013.
24 See The Brookings Institution *Why Wait a Hundred Years? Bridging the gap in Global Education* 2015 www.brookings.edu/research/why-wait-100-years-bridging-the-gap -in-global-education/; and *Learning to Leapfrog,* 2019. www.brookings.edu/resea rch/learning-to-leapfrog/.
25 A long research tradition started in 1934 by Vygotsky (1962).
26 See, for example practitioner research such as https://npjscilearncommunity.nature. com/users/328634-charlotte-wilson/posts/56629-learning-should-be-a-social-activity, and through the work of NOII https://noiie.ca.

20 *The pandemic shock*

27 See Harvard Adult Development Study www.adultdevelopmentstudy.org/.
28 For a discussion of this idea see Achen et al. 2016, and Hannon, 2021. Also Taylor, Matthew. 'Democratic Renewal, or Else ...' *RSA* (blog), 5 April 2016. www. thersa.org/discover/publications-and-articles/matthew-taylor-blog/2016/04/dem ocratic-renewal-or-else.
29 Fielding and Moss, 2011.
30 Apple M., 2007.
31 UNESCO, 2020.

References and further reading

Achen, Christopher H., and Larry M. Bartels. *Democracy for Realists: Why Elections Do Not Produce Responsive Government.* Princeton: Princeton University Press, 2016.

Apple, Michael. Education, markets and an audit culture. *International Journal of Educational Policies,* Vol. 1 (1), 2007, 4–19.

Beare, Hedley. *Creating the FutureSchool.* Abingdon, UK: Routledge and Falmer, 2000.

Caldwell, Brian*et al.Beyond the Self-Managing School.* Melbourne, Australia: Psychology Press, 1998.

Diamond, Jared M. *Guns, Germs, and Steel: The Fates of Human Societies.* New York: Norton, 2005.

Facer, Keri. *Learning Futures, Technology and Social Change.* Abingdon UK: Routledge, 2011.

Fielding, Michael, and Moss P. *Radical Education and the Common School: A Radical Alternative.* Abingdon UK: Routledge, 2011.

Fullan, Michael, and Donnelly K.Alive in the swamp: assessing digital innovations in education. London: *NESTA 2013.* www.nesta.org.uk/report/alive-in-the-swamp -assessing-digital-innovations-in-education.

Gore, Al. *The Future: The Six Drivers of Global Change.* New York: Random House, 2013.

Hannon, Valerie, and Peterson, A.K. *Thrive: The Purpose of Schools in a Changing World.* Cambridge: Cambridge University Press, 2021.

Illych, Ivan. *Deschooling Society.* New York: Harper & Row, 1971.

Miller, Riel. Futures literacy: embracing complexity and using the future, *Ethos,* Issue 10, Oct.2011.

Miller, R. (Ed). *Transforming the Future: Anticipation In the 21st Century,* Abingdon UK: Routledge, 2019.

OECD. Schooling for Tomorrow: What Schools For the Future?Paris: OECD CERI, 2001.

OECD. The Nature of Learning: Using Research To Inspire Practice. Paris: OECD CERI, 2010.

OECD. Innovative Learning Environments. Paris: OECD CERI, 2013.

OECD. Framework for Education and Skills 2030. Paris: OECD, 2018.

OECD. Back to the Future of Education: Four OECD Scenarios for Schooling. Paris: OECD CERI, 2020 (a).

Reimers E. *School is Dead: An Essay On Alternatives in Education.* Harmondsworth UK: Penguin, 1971.

UNESCO. International Commission on The Futures of Education. Education in a Post-COVID world: 9 ideas for public action. Paris: UNESCO, 2020.

Vygotsky, L.S. *Thought and Language.* Cambridge, MA: MIT Press, 1962.

3 Design principles from futures thinking

Change by design

In 1900, fewer than 5% of factories in the US used electric motors for their drive power (despite electric motors having been readily available for over half a century).

The capabilities of the electric motors had not been utilised. Why? Optimising their use meant having smaller individual motors for each worker. Factories needed to spread out to be lighter, airier spaces. But factory design was entrenched.

Then, in 1914, war struck. The costs of labour skyrocketed. Factories needed more productive workers who could work more autonomously. Factories got redesigned and the technology at last got exploited.

The parallels here are obvious – even if the very last metaphor we would want to employ for the school is that of the factory. What is key is the *willingness to redesign*: to think about what is really important and redesign on the basis of the conclusions. The availability of technology is secondary. Applying 21st century technology to the old learning paradigm perpetuates the fundamental flaws. And, whilst there is no guarantee that a crisis brings about fresh thinking, there are plenty of examples where it does. The question is: can the pandemic of 2020 become the catalyst to accelerate fundamental, widespread redesign of the institution of school?

When Seymour Papert, the great educator, mathematician and pioneer of AI was asked what key changes he would make to school systems, he said:

> *Do away with curriculum. Do away with segregation by age. And do away with the idea that there should be uniformity of all schools and of what people learn*[1].

But then, what guides us in the construction of the new? This is the critical role of design principles. In the discipline of design itself, design principles are defined as widely applicable guidelines or considerations, drawn from a variety of disciplines, to be applied with discretion and judgement. They represent the accumulated wisdom of researchers and practitioners. They are sometimes described as "laws with leeway": that is, not rigid or immutable but to be applied with consciousness of context – and always with an eye to the user experience.

Making the translation to the education context, and the task of creating schools for the future, the relevance of this is clear. Looking across the collection of

DOI: 10.4324/9781003244172-3

22 *Design principles from futures thinking*

principles (sometimes described in slightly different language) that emerge from the work of the organisations we have scanned, some key categories emerge. Whilst there are differences of emphasis and expression, it is possible to identify coherent clusters of principles that provide a strong frame within which to develop schools for the future. When combined they indicate a significant break with prevailing models of the school, the artefacts of 19th century thinking and expectations.

What were the functions of the old model?

The idea that children should be brought together, outside their families, and assigned to the care of one or more adults charged with the task of furthering their learning goes back at least as far as ancient Greece, probably earlier. Initially they were exclusively for elites. It was not until the 19th century that schooling became compulsory, overseen by the State. The nature of the 'school' naturally followed its function. No attempt to sketch out the future of this function – and therefore its form – should ignore how those functions have shifted over time. They include:

- Being vehicles of myth transmission
- Protecting and spreading religions
- In the Industrial Revolution, preparing workers with basic literacy who understood their place and could obey instructions
- Cultural transmission – an idea that became explicit in the 19th century through writers such as Matthew Arnold, exhorting schools to transmit "*the best that has been thought and said*". In 1869, School Inspector (as well as poet) Arnold built the case for teaching a canonical body of knowledge, an idea that exerts a powerful pull today.
- Disciplinary scholarship – in the 1890s, Arnold's idea evolved into the notion, codified by the 'Committee of Ten', that high schools should give grounding in key disciplines: nine subject areas creating a template of school timetables persisting to this day.
- Custodial function: providing safe care and custody of children during the working day, especially relevant as women entered the workforce.
- Socialising students into prevailing norms
- Sorting students into vocational pathways
- Acquiring '21st century skills': more complex and sophisticated requirements of workforces needed to be satisfied in post-industrial 'knowledge economies'.
- The vehicle for social mobility, or equity.

Sometimes these functions were made explicit in societal debates: more often they are implicit and taken for granted. But they represent the job we have wanted the schooling system to do for us.

The schools that fortified religions, such as Christianity in the Middle Ages, were established in the buildings already existing and used by those religions, for example the monasteries. Purpose-built schools followed: The Kings School (Canterbury, England) built in 594CE is arguably the oldest continuously operating school in the world. The architecture of schools has naturally aligned to the spirit of the times: the Victorians built schools resembling factories; mid-20th-century schools built of steel and glass looked like office blocks. Of course, not all 'schools' were (or are) building-based. 'Hedge schools' in Ireland operated illegally to give primary rudimentary education to Catholics and other non-conformists. 'Open air' schools (such as Forest Schools) in the Netherlands and Scandinavia are well known, operating mostly in the early years phase. And Australia, of necessity, created the first School of the Air in 1951.

So what is different now?

The functions described above for schools either looked backward – transmitting culture – or were concerned with the present or very immediate future – the demands of economies. It is only relatively recently that educators have taken the view that the gaze needs to be further forward. *It has dawned that we must educate learners for their future, not our past or present.* Furthermore, we must consider very broad aspects of the future, and for a longer time frame.

Various writers have explored different scenarios. Miller and Bentley[2] theorised around variations of the existing functions, and floated some new ones. Schools might dispense with their custodial function, or with the responsibility for screening and sorting students into vocational categories, as these roles come to be taken on by other institutions or organisational systems. They might give up their assumed monopoly on organising formal learning activity, and instead play a role in sustaining and validating much wider networks of learning and knowledge transfer.

What the last decade has thrown up, however, has been a range of organisations that are not just theorising, but are bringing futures thinking to the task of proactively supporting its practical realisation in new forms of the 'school'.

The groundwork has been laid

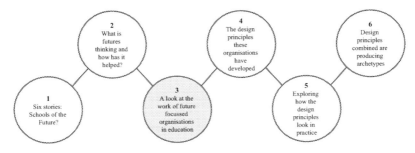

Figure 3.1 Step three

24 *Design principles from futures thinking*

In the last decade an increasing number of organisations have been exploring what schools fit for the future should look like. In this chapter we look at what has emerged from their work, and subsequently how their work has influenced, and been influenced by, great innovative practice.

We have scanned for organisations whose work is distinctive in that it draws explicitly upon futures thinking, and attempts to align ideas about what schools should be to the best evidence about what the future looks like. Of course, this work supplements and builds upon the countless experiments and efforts by individuals and groups who have, ever since mass schooling was created, sought to expand or alter the model.

Naturally the scan cannot claim to be a comprehensive survey: but we are confident that it represents the most prominent organisations focused on this issue. They range from intergovernmental agencies (such as the OECD) to catalytic philanthropy (Chan Zuckerberg) to innovative providers (such as Big Picture Learning). All have learned from the work of individual educators, or groups, who have experimented with models beyond the conventional frame.

Our data set of future-facing organisations contains a disparate set of approaches. Some are research-based (like the OECD's work on *Education and Skills 2030*). Others are invitational — challenge-based prizes for school models of the future (the XQ Institute). Some are focused primarily on capacity building — creating professional development programmes to change educators' thinking and practice (Deep Learning).

What they share is a common set of considerations to guide how schools for the future should be planned. The considerations are:

- The features of the future that evidence and scholarship have been identifying as significant and pivotal
- New knowledge about human learning[3]
- Innovative practice that has demonstrated what is possible, effective and inspiring.

Here is the full set of organisations we reviewed:

- Big Picture Learning
- Carnegie Mellon Eberly Centre
- Chan Zuckerberg Initiative
- The Coalition of Essential School
- Deans for Impact
- Education Reimagined
- Expeditionary Learning
- First Peoples Principles of Learning (Canada)
- The High Tech High Group
- Institute of Applied Neuroscience
- Knowledge Works
- LEAP Innovations
- Learning Frontiers
- Lego Foundation
- New Pedagogies for Deep Learning
- Next Gen Learning
- OECD Innovative Learning Environments 7 Principles
- OECD Education 2030 Learning Framework
- Remake Learning
- Re-school Colorado
- Transcend Education
- Yidan Prize
- XQ Institute

Design principles from futures thinking 25

Readers can of course themselves explore the activities of each of these organisations (see Appendix). All have made important contributions to thinking about learning. However, what is of particular interest for the focus of this book is the extent to which each organisation has alighted on the concept of *design principles* (sometimes going under different labels) as a vital tool in guiding action.

And this has never been more important than at a time when the 2020 pandemic school shutdown forced questions about the role of schools in communities, especially in the light of the contribution that technology can now play. If it is true that this 'great pause' has created the space and the opportunity to reconsider the nature of the institution of 'school', what is to guide us in that quest? Surely this is the point where a considered application of thinking about the future provides – in the terms adopted by the OECD – a 'learning compass'? Combined with an ever-improving knowledge base about the nature of human learning, futures thinking provides the parameters and signposts to the way forward.

Whilst a detailed appreciation of the work of all these organisations is not possible in a book with this scope, nevertheless it may be helpful to give a flavour of how futures thinking, combined with learning research and practical exemplars, has enabled these organisations to codify the work into *design principles* for schools of the future.

With that in mind, we have selected three examples to demonstrate the emergence and reliance on design principles as a foundational concept in planning and executing their future-focused plans.

Knowledge Works

Combining futures thinking, learning research and practical exemplification is a particularly potent formula for distilling valuable knowledge to guide action. KnowledgeWorks is a twenty-year-old foundation in the US, doing exactly that. Early on, it began its forecasts of the future of learning, examining possible futures based on the best analyses that were available. It published the first Future Forecast, Map of Future Forces in 2006. Its fifth Future Forecast, The Future of Learning: Education in the Era of Partners in Code[4] was created in 2016. Each of these forecasts has built upon layers of the previous publications. The most recent explored five drivers of change:

1. Optimised Selves – Discovering new human horizons
2. Labor Relations 2.0 – Negotiating new machine partnerships
3. Alternate Economies – Finding the right niche
4. Smart Transactional Models – Creating self-managing institutions
5. Shifting Landscapes – Innovating in volatile conditions

Briefly, KnowledgeWorks concludes from this analysis that we are rapidly entering a new era in which our economy, our institutions and our societal structures are shifting at an accelerating pace. Our lives will become so

26 Design principles from futures thinking

inextricably linked with our digital companions that we will find ourselves living as partners in code, creating the next generation of human digital co-evolution. Code will become increasingly ingrained in our lives. It will only be noticeable when missing. For KnowledgeWorks the key will be to define how people foster productive relationships with technology that leverage and celebrate the unique contributions of our humanity so that we can thrive amid intensifying complexity.

KnowledgeWorks recognised early that the factory-era education system had to change. It reversed the focus on the needs of the institution, and put learners at the centre. The concept of personalisation became central to its theoretical, advocacy and practical work: it researched, celebrated and advocated for environments that fostered a growth mindset, the cultivation of essential social-emotional skills and student agency, providing opportunities for learners to demonstrate mastery in a variety of ways and make meaningful connections with what they are learning.

The design principles that KnowledgeWorks has evolved flow from this central focus on personalisation, which it defines as:

- Instruction aligned to rigorous academic standards and social-emotional skills students need to be ready for college, career and life
- Customised instruction that allows each student to design learning experiences aligned to his or her interests
- Varied pacing of instruction based on individual student needs, allowing students to accelerate or take additional time based on their level of mastery
- Real-time differentiation of instruction, supports and interventions based on data from formative assessments and student feedback to ensure every student remains on track to graduation.

Access to clear, transferable learning objectives and assessment results so students and families understand what is expected for mastery and advancement.

With some differences in approach and focus, *Education Reimagined* and *Next Gen Learning* are organisations that have adopted similar methodologies to *KnowledgeWorks*, utilising futures thinking to scan for exciting practice and distilling from these overarching principles that appear to be key.

OECD programs: Innovative Learning Environments and Framework for Education and Skills 2030

As an intergovernmental agency, the Organisation for Economic Co-operation and Development (OECD) occupies a very different space. It works to promote "better policies for better lives" but can only work through national

Design principles from futures thinking 27

governments adopting those policies. Its levers have been through research analysis and establishing evidence-based international comparisons. It seeks to be a knowledge hub for data and analysis, and exchange of experiences and "best practice". In education, it established its profile by creating the first reliable international comparison of performance in standardised tests – the Programme for International Assessment (PISA).

The OECD had been starting to expand its focus beyond the assessment of performance based on the old paradigm of schooling when its Centre for Research and Innovation (CERI) embarked on its *Schooling for Tomorrow* project, which by 2005 had expanded to 11 countries. As we described in Chapter 2, this work was founded in the methodology of scenario planning based on futures trend analysis. It took a set of currently powerful trends and combined them in various ways to generate a set of alternative futures that were internally coherent and consistent with the current direction of travel. *What Schools for the Future?* theorised the possibilities.

The successor work was the *Innovative Learning Environments* programme begun in 2008. This was a primarily research-based initiative, and perhaps was the first to synthesise a set of principles for learning in the future. The principles the project identified were:

1   Learners at the centre
2   The social nature of learning
3   Emotions are integral to learning
4   Recognising individual differences
5   Stretching all students
6   Assessment for learning
7   Building horizontal connections

The OECD achieved considerable traction in some countries with this work, and its influence can be seen directly in some of the policies and practices adopted by the most high-performing systems.

The piece that the OECD then developed was to blend the research focus with a futures-thinking lens, combined with practice examples drawn from across its member states. The Education and Skills 2030[5] project was established in 2015, and by 2020 was the most supported education program the OECD was running. The key shift was to start to explore explicitly what the purpose of learning/schooling needed to be in the future: to construct the "future we want". But to get there, the organisation commissioned, from across its many assets, analyses of likely futures trends and their implications for humanity and the development of human capital. This welcome breadth of view suggested that the "future we want" needed to be across a range of domains. The OECD suggested the canvas shown in Figure 3.2.

28 Design principles from futures thinking

> Competencies that students need to **shape their future** for better lives in 2030.... **What are the futures they want to create?**

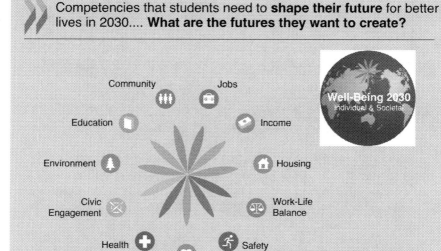

Figure 3.2 OECD future landscape

Interestingly, the OECD incorporated into their work not just analyses from trend data and futures thinkers, but also samples of inputs from young people themselves, in terms of the kind of future they wanted to create. Hence the future was conceived not as something immutable or anyhow beyond human control – in which case the best thing we could do would be to help young people cope. Rather, that the future – in spite of the clear trajectories of trends – could be influenced and created. The area in which young people felt most strongly about this, unsurprisingly, was the climate crisis. This naturally influenced the kinds of design principles that the OECD eventually incorporated into its Framework. The principal effect of this was to highlight the importance of promoting agency. Earlier work on personalisation, whilst it focused on individual's needs and talents, did not necessarily invoke the importance of enabling young people to take reflective action in pursuit of their goals and objectives – which is at the heart of the idea of agency.

The First People's Principles of Learning

The third example drawn from our dataset of organisations looked not only to the future, but also to what must not be lost from the past. In a sense this is about looking forward, informed by the wisdom of the past; it is about rediscovering things that have been lost in the industrialised model of schools and learning, which are precious. Futures thinkers are now acutely aware that, if we are to survive as a species – for the stakes are as high as that – we need to rediscover wisdom about humanity in relation to our planet and each other that has become buried.

In this spirit, British Columbia (BC), Canada, has incorporated the First People's Principles of Learning into its futures-facing curriculum introduced in 2016. Developed by the First Nations' Education Steering Committee (FNESC)[6] and the cooperation of many indigenous educators, the principles seek to synthesise deep traditions of pedagogy that have a profound resonance with new understandings about humans' place in the world, and our potential future.

There is a striking similarity between some of the Principles in the FNESC (and now BC) work and those that emerged from the OECD work. To take two:

- Learning ultimately supports the well-being of the self, the family, the community, the land, the spirits and the ancestors.
- Learning is holistic, reflexive, reflective, experiential and relational (focused on connectedness, on reciprocal relationships, and a sense of place).

The first is congruent with the OECD's emphasis on the wide scope of well-being as a goal. The second reflects the qualities that the OECD identified in its commissioned research on powerful learning.

Design principles – a synthesis and overview

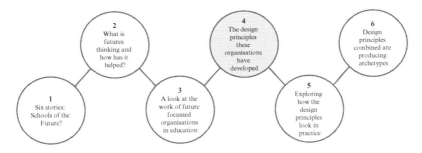

Figure 3.3 Step four

30 *Design principles from futures thinking*

Looking across the work of all the 23 organisations we surveyed, we found design principles falling into three categories or clusters:

- The *values* that future schools ought to manifest
- The *operational philosophy* that demonstrates those values in practice
- The *learner's experience* of the above

Design principles 1: Values

Our surveyed organisations all privileged some key values for schools in their work. Perhaps this reflects the fact that something important has been lost – a north star. This is not to deny that many school leaders do already try to focus on this issue – in some contexts, finding it very difficult to do so in the prevailing accountability regimes they inhabit.

In looking at the initiatives in our data set we found the following design principles relating to the concept of values:

- *Purpose driven*: Futureschools are themselves focused on the purpose of both individual and collective thriving, and on helping their learners to acquire personal purpose: building their 'why?'
- *Equity-focused*: such schools should work to address inequities and social justice, and help young people to do so.
- *Promoting identity*: this principle suggests that each learner's social and cultural identity must be nurtured, cultivating a sense of belonging and value.
- *Strength-based*: this principle asserts that the school recognises, celebrates and builds from each (and every) individual's existing assets.

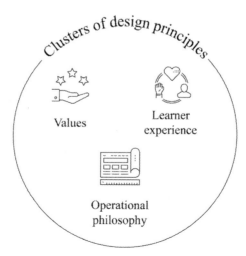

Figure 3.4 Clusters of design principles

Design principles from futures thinking 31

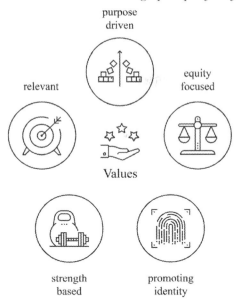

Figure 3.5 Design principles on values

- *Relevant*: this proposes that learning be relevant to the local and global community; "work that matters" should be an important feature.

Design principles 2: Operational philosophy

Values mean nothing if their force is not felt in translation to practice. So the organisations we looked at had assembled clear principles in this domain. They were:

- *Learning focused*: learning is at the heart – so understanding how learning happens, the very best in learning sciences and research underpin developments – and this applies to the adult learning (of all staff) too. This is a critically important principle: and it is not axiomatic by any means in all schools.
- *Flexible/dynamic*: the school should design and iterate different modes of teaching and learning to meet the evolving needs of learners and the wider world. In an age of disruption this is an imperative – as schools found out in 2020.
- *Technology enhanced*: future schools use technology extensively and responsibly to liberate learning, amplify effective and diverse modalities, and to enable both personalisation and collaboration.
- *Ecosystemic*: this principle asserts the school should be seriously porous with many active partners in organising learning. It will be deeply connected to its local community (and also to the global community through technology) to provide richer learning experiences and diverse pathways for learners.

32 *Design principles from futures thinking*

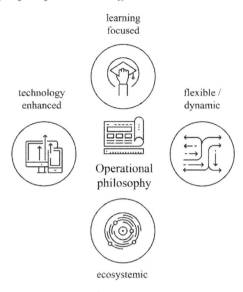

Figure 3.6 Design principles on operational philosophy

Design principles 3: Learner experience

Schools may set out to operationalise their values authentically, but a *design* principle will always be highly attentive to the user experience. What is it like to be on the receiving end? We found a strong awareness of this issue in many of the organisations we surveyed, and it is reflected in the following principles:

- *Personalised*: the learner's experience relates to their personal needs, passions, development and purposes. These are at the centre: not the institution, the teacher, or external bodies of knowledge.
- *Integrated*: the learner experiences meaning through learning that transcends siloes, building relevant connections within and between disciplines. This is about utilising many forms: disciplinary; intra-disciplinary; cross-disciplinary.
- *Inclusive*: the culture is experienced as respectful and welcoming.
- *Relational*: individuals are known, good relationships are the basis for deep learning. Collaboration is the norm.
- *Empowering*: Futureschools build and leverage learner agency (or self-direction), providing opportunities for learners to take increasing responsibility and ownership over their learning.

These are the design principles we uncovered when exploring the work of future-focused organisations. They may appear to be highly abstract: they do not specify particular pedagogies, for example, nor curriculum frameworks, nor approaches to assessment. But they can provide the future-focused basis

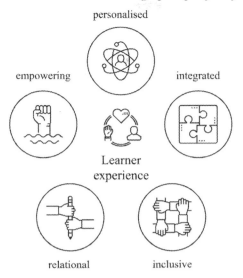

Figure 3.7 Design principles on learner experience

for taking decisions on those questions. Taken in combination they have led to the construction of sets of particular pedagogical approaches, or repertoires. The resulting repertoires (or mix of teaching practices) include: design thinking, game-based learning, nature-based learning, project-based learning, phenomenon-based learning, passion projects, service learning and yes, our old friend direct instruction too, which continues to have a place[7].

In a sense that is the point. The key task is how the principles are selected and combined: how they are expressed in practice may lead to a diversity of models, although sharing a similar DNA. Context, culture and place are so important. So is history. A reminder of the definition of design principles offered above: "laws with leeway". They cannot be rigid or immutable but need to be applied with consciousness of context.

These design principles are being put into practice in schools across the world in an effort to equip learners not just to cope with the future, but to shape and inhabit it. These will be the key take-away messages for educators looking for guides to the new paradigm. The design principles adopted impact how the basic architecture (or 'grammar'[8]) of schooling is changed: how time, space, tech and people are deployed: how schooling is reshaping itself to fit the contours of a changing world.

To explore how this looks we constructed a large database of such schools. Over the next three chapters we turn to the practice of some schools engaging deeply in this work.

Notes

1 www.sfgate.com/news/article/SUNDAY-INTERVIEW-Seymour-Papert-Computers-In-2856685.php.
2 Miller and Bentley, 2006.
3 Particularly insights drawn from researchers such as Willingham, 2010.
4 https://knowledgeworks.org/resources/forecast-5.
5 See OECD op. cit., 2018.
6 First Nations Education Steering Committee of British Columbia www.fnesc.ca.
7 For a full discussion of the 'pedagogy packages' that have now been developed see LearnLife's overview at www.learnlife.com/methodologies.
8 Tyzack, David, and Tobin, W., "The 'Grammar' of Schooling: Why Has It Been So Hard to Change?" *American Educational Research Journal Vol. 31, No. 3 (Autumn, 1994), pp. 453–479.*

References and further reading

Claxton, Guy. *What's the Point of School? Rediscovering The Heart Of Education.* Reprint edition. Oxford: Oneworld Publications, 2008.

Miller, Riel, and Bentley, T. *Unique Creation.* Nottingham: National College for School Leadership, 2006.

Postman, Neil. *The End of Education: Redefining the Value of School.* 1st Vintage Books Ed edition. New York: Vintage Books, 1996.

Richardson, Will. *Why School? How Education Must Change When Learning and Information Are Everywhere.* e-book. TED, 2012. www.amazon.co.uk/Why-School-Education-Information-Everywhere-ebook/dp/B00998J5YQ.

Slayback, Zachary. *The End of School: Reclaiming Education from the Classroom.* Remnant Publishing, 2016.

Stein, Zachary. *Education in a Time Between Worlds: Essays on the Future of Schools, Technology, and Society.* Bright Alliance, 2019.

Willingham, Daniel T. *Why Don't Students Like School? A Cognitive Scientist Answers Questions About How the Mind Works and What It Means for the Classroom,* 1st edition. San Francisco, CA: Jossey Bass, 2010.

4 Design principles in action
Values

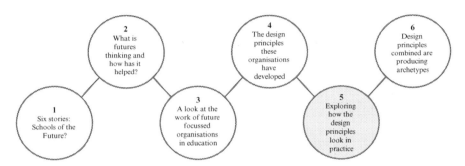

Figure 4.1 Step 5

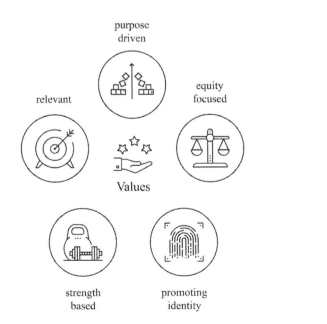

Figure 4.2 Design principles – values

DOI: 10.4324/9781003244172-4

36 *Design principles in action: Values*

In this chapter, and in the two that follow, we explore what the adoption of the future-focused design principles in schools looks like in practice.

Like the exemplar or archetypal schools in Chapter 1, the schools described in these chapters have many compelling features. However, on this occasion we shine a light on a single design principle and explore its effects on curriculum, pedagogy and assessment, relationships and culture, learning spaces and so on.

By looking at each school through the lens of just one design principle we can 'zoom in' on specific features of each school, to bring each design principle to life. We also get to tell stories about more extraordinary schools, which we hope will inspire and engage too.

Here is a reminder of the five design principles that our research identified in the cluster relating to values.

Design principle 1: Purpose driven

Futureschools are themselves focused on the purpose of both individual and collective thriving, and on helping their learners to acquire personal purpose: building their 'why?'

Purpose driven: Arts education and social action – a school "made for this moment"[1]

New Roads School, Santa Monica, California, USA

On 20 January 2021, the inauguration of the 46th President of the United States of America was stopped in its tracks by a 22-year-old, black, female poet from Los Angeles. It was a most extraordinary moment. Amanda Gorman's poem *The Hill We Climb*[2], completed two weeks previously in the hours after the storming of the Capitol by supporters of the outgoing President, electrified an audience of America's most powerful people and captured the attention of millions around the world[3]. By 22 January, Gorman's two books were the number one and two bestselling books in the USA and her social media following had grown from just over 100,000 to over two million[4].

What's interesting about this story, aside of course from Gorman's brilliant performance on the day, is that at 22 she was already a published poet, a Harvard Graduate and the USA's first National Youth Poet Laureate[5]. She is also a twin. Amanda's sister Gabrielle is a graduate of UCLA Film School, an activist and a successful filmmaker.

Amanda and Gabrielle, whose mother is a single parent and middle-school teacher, attended New Roads School in Santa Monica, from kindergarten to graduation. Lines from Amanda's now globally recognised poem resonate powerfully with the ethos and mission of her school:

We the people of New Roads liberate young individuals through the pursuit of justice, equity, and opportunity; raising generations of powerfully compassionate advocates in an intellectual habitat driven by authentic diversity — ultimately empowering them to disrupt systems that produce inequality and build a more just future.

New Roads School Mission Statement[6]

New Roads School was opened in 1995 shortly after the Rodney King riots in Los Angeles. Its founder, Paul Cummins, then Principal of a successful private school elsewhere in the County, had the idea of taking over a run-down public elementary school in a mostly low-income neighbourhood and inviting parents on the waiting list of his previous school to instead choose New Roads.

Cummins' plan was to charge wealthy parents $10,000 per year for 50% of the places at the new school and for the remaining 50% to go to children from the local community, funded by the State at a much lower $4000 per student. This would create a $2.8m budget for 400 students to provide a high-quality education in a school that was socio-economically, racially and culturally integrated, unique to and reflective of Los Angeles. Cummins' vision was for "a center (sic) of progressive education and community service—an entirely new education model, a unique community of rich and poor, Caucasian, African American, Hispanic and Asian. This community would reflect the true diversity of the city as a whole"[78].

This radical funding and enrolment model struggled to gain the support of parents to begin with. Cummins believes that, as challenging for parents as the emphasis on social action was the school's commitment to education through the arts. Himself a poet, Cummins had successfully brought the arts into the heart of the curriculum at his previous school, which largely attracted children whose parents were involved in the film and creative industries. For the prospective families of New Roads School, however, a focus on art education felt frivolous:

To many of them the arts were a frill, a pleasant diversion perhaps, but a deflection from the real business of the Three Rs. I knew instantly and intuitively that this attitude did a disservice to children. The joys of childhood—inventing games, make-believe, play, storytelling, and fantasy—are as natural to children as breathing. To do anything but give children full and untrammeled encouragement to express their gifts and forces of their inner worlds is not only misinformed but harmful.

Paul Cummins, Founder, New Roads School[9]

Today New Roads serves 520 students, around 40% of whom receive support for their fees: a direct and explicit redistribution of the wealth of full fee-paying families, who want their children to be part of a vibrant community that sees diversity as strength. People of colour make up 40% of students and 34% of the teaching staff.[10]

For Luthern Williams, Principal at New Roads School since 2015, the school's commitment to inclusion and social justice is at the heart of everything. Speaking about a series of discussions held at New Roads School following the killing of George Floyd in May 2020, Williams said:

38 *Design principles in action: Values*

> *At our school, it's really not about indoctrinating people to believe one way or another but about getting our kids the critical tools to make mindful decisions, where they're thinking about the impact of their words and actions on others. We also know that kids are, through their social conditioning, already getting information about race and understanding what that means in who they are and how society assigns value to that*[11].

And for Aaliyah Mack, a senior at New Roads, the approach seems to be working:

> *The school is teaching us to speak up. The school is teaching us that we are the change that the world so desperately needs, and I think that when we have an environment like that, that's constantly encouraging, it pushes us to want to do better.*
>
> Aaliyah Mack, 17, New Roads School student[12]

Design principle 2: Equity-focused

Such schools work to address inequities and social justice and help young people to do so.

Equity-focused: Confronting racial inequality and amplifying minority voices

School 21, London, UK

Every Monday in School 21, as part of their well-being curriculum, learners throughout the school take part in assemblies that kick-start a series of discussions on controversial social issues that unfold during the week. This 'well-being curriculum' is designed to help children to understand the world around them and make sense of what they feel about the things they see happening. Children as young as six years old tackle questions such as *Should boys play with dolls?* And *Does skin colour tell you much about a person on the inside?*

> *Wellbeing is not judging people from the outside but from the inside. It teaches you things about being respectful to others*[13].
>
> Aaishah, Year 3

There is a strong focus on empathy and fairness and challenging assumptions and misconceptions, in particular about race. School 21 is in Newham, a part of East London, UK that is ethnically diverse and socially disadvantaged. The school consistently and systematically celebrates diversity and highlights aspects of culture – dress, food, festivals – to help children to understand and learn to appreciate and see strength in difference.

The well-being curriculum supports learners safely to unpack and explore fears and concerns they might have or hear from others – dangerous ideas that might otherwise cause damage – in discussion groups based on the Philosophy for Children (P4C) model[14]. In discussion, learners choose an inquiry question to investigate and debate together, which helps them to explore in depth a presenting social issue.

For Peter Hyman, Co-founder and Chief Executive of the group of schools of which School 21 is a part, challenging and supporting learners to become advocates for fairness is critical to securing a better future:

> *With extreme politics on the march and the potential for an era of 'illiberal' democracy to sweep the west, how do we teach young people that tolerance is a quality to be prized, not discarded when times get tough?*[15]

> Peter Hyman, 2018

For Hyman and his team, Nelson Mandela's belief in education as *"the most powerful weapon which you can use to change the world"*[16] is a call to action; a reminder that schools prepare learners not just *for* the future, but to shape it. If a fairer world is what we seek then young people need to be agents for equity.

Fundamental to School 21's approach to promoting agency amongst learners is their oracy programme. Partly this is about equity for learners themselves. A higher-than-average number of learners in School 21 come from ethnic minority backgrounds where English is not their first language, or from low-income families, or both. The links between speech and language difficulties – often undiagnosed – through to impaired life chances have been well documented and disproportionately affect disadvantaged children. By age three children from low-income families will have heard 30 million fewer words spoken at home, where 98% of language acquisition happens in the early years. And of young people aged 16 to 24 in youth custody in the UK, 60% have speech and language difficulties[17].

Teachers in School 21 actively support 'noisy classrooms' in which speaking and listening is given equal status with reading and writing. Evaluations of Voice 21, School 21's oracy programme, demonstrate significant learning gains in other areas, as well as increasing oracy skills.

The ability to express themselves empowers learners to ensure they are heard and understood, first by their peers and their teachers in school and later by their families, in their communities and in the world[18].

Oracy is a powerful driver of social mobility and demand is on the increase. In 2020, the Voice 21 programme was shared through a non-profit social enterprise with 1100 partner schools across England.

Design principle 3: Promoting identity

This principle suggests that each learner's social and cultural identity must be nurtured, cultivating a sense of belonging and value.

40   *Design principles in action: Values*

Promoting identity: Valuing diversity and growing empathy

Riverside School, Ahmedabad, India

Kiran Bir Sethi the founder of Riverside School in Ahmedabad, India, came into education with a designer's mindset, determined to create an engaging and empowering learning environment for her young son, who was becoming disillusioned with school at an early age. Drawing on her design training, Sethi's focus in conceiving her school was not: *What is the curriculum and how should we teach it?* But: *Who are the learners and what do they need to learn?*

A focus on learners – their strengths, interests and needs – led Sethi inevitably to contemplate the implications for learning of the unique challenges and opportunities that each learner faces and the diversity of experience of learners and their communities, which follow them into school. Here too, Sethi drew on her own experience of arriving at design school where, for the first time, she met people whose lives and perspectives were vastly different from her own.

> *I was awed by the sheer diversity in religion, culture, demographics and sexuality on the campus. It was here that I began to believe in inclusion as a right and not the privilege of a select few*[19].

Kiran Bir Sethi, 2018

Through their student admissions and teacher recruitment policies, and over a period of ten years, Riverside explicitly set out to create a 'mini India' amongst the 390 students in their school[20], ensuring representation from all communities, demographics, religious affiliations and gender and welcoming learners with special needs "beyond any labels and biases".[21]

With diversity and inclusion so prominent in the school's design and ethos it is perhaps unsurprising that identity soon became an explicit focus for learning, and Riverside's commitment to inclusion found expression in their Inclusive Campus Programme (ICP).

Centring on nine aspects of identity, the ICP is made up of a range of workshops and experiences that continue throughout a student's time at Riverside. The nine aspects, categorised under the headings of mind, body and heritage are:

- Mind – personality, gender and orientation
- Body – ability, age, appearance
- Heritage – religions and belief, race and ethnicity, socioeconomic class.

Awareness, compassion and engagement are at the heart of the ICP[22]. From stories that challenge gender stereotypes for younger children to intentional conversations between a gay teacher and older students; from collaborative redesign by students of school spaces, to accommodate a wheelchair when a disabled student joined the school, to regular visits to heritage sites and culturally significant spaces around the city; the ICP explicitly and systematically engages

Design principles in action: Values 41

students with alternative perspectives and experiences to challenge them to reflect deeply on their own identity and the role they might play in the world.

As learners progress through the school, the ethos of inclusion and the exploration of identity expands beyond the school walls and out into the real world, to support learners to contemplate what other people's lives are like and how the privilege – not the entitlement – of an education might equip them as Riverside graduates to help others. Learners are encouraged to think of themselves as individuals in the world; agents with skills and purpose and a will to change things for the better for others. "Doing good and doing well" is the Riverside mantra. Learners stay in rural communities where the relative luxury of city living – sanitation, technology, transport – are missing from everyday life. They immerse themselves in alternative realities, learning how agricultural workers and craftspeople make a living. And how a life without material wealth might be enriching in other ways.

In their final year, learners assume responsibility for leading a real and urgent change, becoming the CEO for a changemaker programme to make a positive difference in people's lives. This leadership development is the final stage in growing their confidence and humility to take on ethical and practical challenges as adults and to become a force for good in the world.

None of the focus and time spent on identity comes at the expense of academic excellence. Riverside students have consistently outperformed the top ten schools in Math, Science and English and the school has been ranked the No.1 Day School in Gujarat for several years[23].

> ### Design principle 4: Strength-based
>
> This principle asserts that the school recognises, celebrates and builds from each (and every) individual's existing assets.

Strength-based: Learners uncovering their superpowers

Design39Campus, California, USA

In 2014, Design39Campus became the 39th school to open in the Powey District in San Diego, California. Twice oversubscribed from the outset, D39C is a thriving community of 1100 K-8 learners "changing the way we do school[24]."

At the heart of the school is a learning model that uses design thinking to place students at the centre and organise learning around their interests. Based on research indicating that students who think their teacher knows their strengths are twenty times more likely to be engaged in their learning, D39C takes a strength-based approach to supporting learners to discover and explore their passions and interests.

At the beginning of the school year, learners complete an online programme called Thrively, which evaluates their personal strengths and interests – learners call

42   *Design principles in action: Values*

this uncovering their superpowers – and returns an 'uplifting' individual strengths profile, suggesting themes, projects and skills to pursue during the year[25].

All teachers and learners explicitly nurture a growth mindset; believing that intelligence is not fixed and that everyone can grow smarter through effort. Based on the work of Carol Dweck[26], Growth Mindset is one of eight foundations that inform the design and operation of the school[27]. Persistence and tenacity are seen as keys to achieving great things and failure is viewed positively, as a chance to learn from mistakes[28]. The school seeks to grow learners' confidence, grit, gratitude and purpose through developing a growth mindset.

Throughout the year, in addition to a core curriculum that centres on design thinking, learners are encouraged to try out a wide range of new experiences through the school's Exploration enrichment programme. Learning a new skill such as playing a musical instrument, creating visual art or making something 3D are ways to broaden learners' horizons and introduce them to new interests they might otherwise never even think to try.

To complement the breadth of the Exploration programme, learners also take part each year in several 'Deep Dives'; extended projects that link their learning in school to the real world of the community, environment or business.

This interest-led approach is intended to support children to find and pursue their passions, creating lifelong learners with a love of inquiry.

In 2018, Design39Campus was ranked as the highest performing middle school in its district and recorded the highest score on every key indicator of school climate and student well-being[29].

Design principle 5: Relevant

This principle proposes that learning be relevant to the local and global community; "work that matters" should be an important feature.

Relevant: A school about and for its community

Crosstown High School, Tennessee, USA

In 2018 in downtown Memphis, Crosstown High School opened with 125 ninth grade students selected by lottery. In 2019, a further 148 joined the school. Fully populated the school is designed to serve 550 students. The lottery entry means that school demographics reflect those in the neighbourhood: half are Black/African American and one third White; 41% qualify for free meals and 11% receive additional education support. The school is "diverse by design" an important statement in a city where neighbourhoods and schools are often segregated[30].

So far so familiar, but Crosstown High is unlike any other school in Memphis. It is located on the fourth and fifth floors of a redeveloped warehouse in the city centre, co-located with arts organisations and healthcare providers, a FedEx Office,

Design principles in action: Values   43

six restaurants, small businesses, a Credit Union, juice bar, coffee shops and so on. The Crosstown Concourse is a "vertical urban village," a thriving commercial, public and residential centre, with a school – Crosstown High – at its heart[31].

Location is critical to understanding the relevance of Crosstown High for Memphis and vice versa. Being part of a multi-million-dollar urban regeneration programme sets the scene and the expectation for what students at Crosstown High can and must achieve on behalf of their communities.

They are the next generation, part of a grand narrative and ambition for Memphis, in which they will thrive and lead.

> *To prepare students to understand and pursue solutions to the challenges faced by our city and the world, and to give students the confidence to be agents of positive change, now and in the future.*
>
> Crosstown High School mission[32]

This explicit connection to their community and to the future is made manifest in the Crosstown High model of learning, which is experiential, inquiry-oriented and project-based. Learning is organised around a set of competencies, which include: collaborate on teams; learn from the past; engage as a citizen; and build community[33].

Alongside team-taught interdisciplinary school-based learning, students spend two hours every day learning beyond the traditional boundaries of school. Being in the Concourse means students can work alongside professionals, entrepreneurs and service providers to access a wide variety of work-based learning opportunities in hospitality, in business and finance, in performing arts, and social and health care.

Students also undertake community projects, for instance "What challenges exist in Memphis neighborhoods and how can we design or adapt solutions to address them?" This was a ninth-grade project in 2018, meanwhile in tenth grade, students developed a game to simulate class and gender issues in real life, for instance in company hiring practices and the criminal justice system[34].

Although assessment is mainly by presentation and looks very different in Crosstown from other high schools, Crosstown students still take part in external state exams, where in 2018 they outperformed students from other schools by as much as three times[35].

Many schools claim to be values-led. In this chapter, we have shown what it really means when a school makes a value (or set of them) utterly intrinsic to what it is about. We have seen what is taught and learned, and how and where learning happens are influenced by the values that the adults in the school hold, and their hopes for the values that are being modelled for and grown in their learners.

Next, we explore how the authentic adoption of design principles around operational philosophy changes schools' routines and culture.

44 *Design principles in action: Values*

Notes

1 New Roads School Mission Statement, www.newroads.org/about/mission.
2 Amanda Gorman, *The Hill We Climb*, New York: Viking, 2019.
3 Liesl Schillinger, "How Amanda Gorman became the voice of a new American Era," *The Guardian*, January 22, 2021 www.theguardian.com/books/2021/jan/22/how-amanda-gorman-became-the-voice-of-a-new-american-era.
4 Joe Price, *Complex*, "22-Year-Old Poet and Activist Amanda Gorman Gets Major Praise After Inaugural Poem" January 20, 2021 www.complex.com/life/2021/01/amanda-gorman-inaugural-poem-reactions/.
5 Study International, "The education of Amanda Gorman, first National Youth Poet Laureate and inauguration show-stopper" January 21, 2021 www.studyinternational.com/news/amanda-gorman-education-school/.
6 New Roads School Mission Statement www.newroads.org/about/mission.
7 Jay Matthews, "Amanda Gorman's private school: Mix of rich, poor, arts and social action," *The Washington Post*, May 22, 2021 www.washingtonpost.com/local/education/new-roads-school-amanda-gorman/2021/05/21/36d9dd48-b98c-11eb-a5fe-bb49dc89a248_story.html.
8 Sky News, "Inauguration poet Amanda Gorman's ex-teacher says she's incredibly driven to transform the world" January 2021 www.youtube.com/watch?v=ef1PzpVe_ZY.
9 Cummins, Paul, *Confessions of a Headmaster*, (Pasadena: Xeno Books, 2015) in Jay Matthews, "Amanda Gorman's private school: Mix of rich, poor, arts and social action," *The Washington Post*, May 22, 2021 www.washingtonpost.com/local/education/new-roads-school-amanda-gorman/2021/05/21/36d9dd48-b98c-11eb-a5fe-bb49dc89a248_story.html.
10 New Roads School "Quick Facts" www.newroads.org/about/quick-facts–accreditation.
11 Koko Mcoboy "New Roads School in Santa Monica holds discussions about racism with students K12" FOX11, Los Angeles, December 7, 2020 www.foxla.com/news/new-roads-school-in-santa-monica-holds-discussions-about-racism-with-students-k-12.
12 Ibid.
13 Edutopia "Teaching Wellbeing: Helping Students Tackle Social Issues" September 15, 2016 www.youtube.com/watch?v=nralkrM43uQ&feature=emb_title.
14 Steve Williams "A brief history of p4c, especially in the UK" https://p4c.com/wp-content/uploads/2016/07/History-of-P4C.pdf.
15 Peter Hyman "It's time for a real revolution in Britain's schools" *The Guardian*, February 26, 2017 www.theguardian.com/education/2017/feb/26/revolution-in-uk-schools.
16 Susan Ratcliffe (Ed.) "Oxford Essential Quotations (5th Edition)" Oxford: OUP, Online Edition, 2017 www.oxfordreference.com/view/10.1093/acref/9780198184373 0.001.0001/q-oro-ed5-00007046.
17 Karen Bryan, Gillian Garvani, Juliette Gregory and Karen Kilner "Language difficulties and criminal justice: the need for earlier identification." *International Journal of Language and Communication Disorders*, 50 (6), 763–775, 2015 https://shura.shu.ac.uk/10341/2/Bryan%20-%20IJDLC__paper_amends%20march%20%2015.pdf.
18 Oracy 21 "Oracy helps me to learn because it helps me feel more confident" 2020 https://voice21.org/impacts/oracy-helps-me-to-learn-because-it-helps-me-feel-more-confident/.
19 Kiran Bir Sethi "Dear Teachers, Here's How We Can Create an Inclusive Culture for All Students" The Better India, November 2, 2018 www.thebetterindia.com/163007/inclusive-culture-education-riverside-school-ahmedabad/.
20 Education World "The Riverside School, Ahmedabad, 2021" www.educationworld.in/the-riverside-school-ahmedabad/.

21 www.thebetterindia.com/163007/inclusive-culture-education-riverside-school-ahm
edabad/.
22 Riverside School, Inclusive Campus Program, 2021 http://icp.schoolriverside.com/.
23 Varkey Foundation Global Teacher Prize: Kiran Bir Sethi, 2018 www.globaltea
cherprize.org/person?id=2399.
24 ABC 10 News San Diego, "Design39 Campus Getting Ready to Open" August 12,
2014 www.youtube.com/watch?v=Obdg9mxMMJM.
25 Thrively website www.thrively.com/.
26 Dweck, Carol S. PhD, "Mindset: The New Psychology of Success", London:
Random House, 2006.
27 Design39 website "Growth Mindset" Growth Mindset — Design39Campus.
28 Fleming, Nora "Designing a Public School from Scratch" September 19, 2018,
Edutopia, Schools that Work www.edutopia.org/school/design-39-campus.
29 Ibid.
30 Bauman, Caroline "Crosstown High School loses principal after student walkout –
its second principal to go in two years" October 2, 2019, Chalkbeat https://tn.cha
lkbeat.org/2019/10/2/21108959/crosstown-high-school-loses-principal-after-
student-walkout-its-second-principal-to-go-in-two-years.
31 XQ SuperSchools "Crosstown High School" https://assets.ctfassets.net/
35eubtuv0bcm/2xr2DvzK1i04oAya0cSgUM/519d8032f908b737d92bb8d5ba58cec0/
190815_School_PDFs_Crosstown.pdf.
32 Van Der Ark, Tom "Crosstown High: Innovative Memphis School in a Vertical Urban
Village" February 28, 2020 www.forbes.com/sites/tomvanderark/2020/02/28/cross
town-high-innovative-memphis-school-in-a-vertical-urban-village/?sh=10d0883c551c.
33 Crosstown High Website "Competencies" 2020 www.crosstownhigh.org/comp
etencies.
34 Van Der Ark, Tom "Crosstown High: Innovative Memphis School in a Vertical Urban
Village" February 28, 2020 www.forbes.com/sites/tomvanderark/2020/02/28/cross
town-high-innovative-memphis-school-in-a-vertical-urban-village/?sh=10d0883c551c.
35 About 45% of its students were proficient in English I, while 62.5% were proficient
in geometry. That compares with Shelby County Schools' averages of 16.5% proficiency in English I and 17.5% in geometry. Bauman, Caroline " Crosstown High
students walk out of class to call for stronger diversity efforts, bolder innovation"
Chalkbeat, September 20, 2019 in https://eu.usatoday.com/story/news/2019/09/
20/crosstown-high-students-walk-out-call-change-school/2388235001/.

5 Design principles in action
Operational philosophy

In the previous chapter we explored schools that exemplify the cluster of design principles centring on values. The fundamental question that those example schools address is: What should The FutureSchool be for? What is its purpose?

Turning to the operational philosophy design principles, we look at the question of *how* The FutureSchool should work.

The four design principles that our research identified in this cluster are shown in Figure 5.1.

None of these foci is exclusive. Here, perhaps more than in either of the other two chapters, we see schools combining design principles, for example using enhanced technology to make access to learning flexible and dynamic. Or creating learning that is flexible and dynamic to fulfil a role in a vibrant learning ecosystem. Indeed, their power is enhanced by operating interactively.

It may be that some of these principles appear too obvious or axiomatic. Are not all schools, by definition, learning focused? The truth is, in the sense in which this principle is meant, they are not.

Where these example schools differ is in the rigour and consistency with which the design principles have been applied. They pay forensic attention to the detail of what, for instance, being learning focused means for how a school works; instead of, say, being focused on a specific part of the curriculum or on behaviour. That means becoming and remaining informed by the latest research on learning, how the brain works, and how this knowledge base is reflected in practice.

Consequently, the adults who work in these schools are, or have become, experts in the design principle that underpins their operational philosophy.

Design principle 6: Learning focused

Learning is at the heart – understanding how learning happens, the very best in learning sciences and research underpin developments – and this applies to adult learning (of all staff) too.

DOI: 10.4324/9781003244172-5

Design principles in action: Operational philosophy 47

Learning focused: Explicit, research-informed design of student and teacher learning, Latitude High School, Oakland, USA

Latitude High School is a radical charter school in Oakland, the city with the largest percentage of low-achieving schools in California, USA.[1]. Opening in 2018 with just 50 students, Latitude has grown fast and, in 2020, 360 learners were enrolled, 65% of whom were Latino and 25% African American[2].

Founded by, Lillian Hsu, Principal and John Bosselman, Director of Instruction, both of whom previously led schools in the award-winning[3] High Tech High network in San Diego[4], Latitude High School's operational philosophy is informed by a deep understanding of the science of learning and what it takes to help all young people, with a wide range of experiences and starting points, to learn effectively.

Learning at Latitude is project based and real world and takes place in a variety of settings in and out of school.

In three Studios, learners focus on humanities, mathematics, and science and design. Working in small groups, they complete interdisciplinary and purposeful projects of value to the community of Oakland, for example in the design studio learners might work on developing an autonomous vehicle for seniors who can no longer drive, while in the humanities studio others create a podcast about homelessness in the city. As well as their teachers, learners are supported and assessed in their projects by industry experts and community leaders relevant to their project focus.

Problem solving and real-world learning, both examples of experiential learning, are Latitude's chosen strategies for supporting learners to acquire

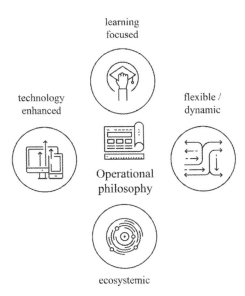

Figure 5.1 Design principles – operational philosophy

48 *Design principles in action: Operational philosophy*

adaptive expertise[5], the ability to apply learned knowledge and skills flexibly and creatively in different situations, also known as transfer[6].

Whereas text-based and rote-learning strategies such as note taking, summarising, and training working memory are highly effective for surface learning for virtually all learners, teachers at Latitude know that deep learning and transfer require more complex, multifaceted pedagogical approaches including action and experiential learning. These approaches require learners to be self-regulating and have high levels of metacognition[7] and what is learned is determined less by teachers and more by context and learners' passions and interests[8].

Latitude invests significantly in supporting learners to discover their passions and interests as part of their commitment to optimising learner engagement and motivation through projects and through extended learning opportunities, which include a wide range of out-of-school experiences.

Through regular shadowing, site visits and internships learners explore ways to pursue their passions and interests in professional environments. They spend time in large companies and with individual practitioners learning not just what qualifications they might need but also what it means to work in a sector or industry, from people who have been successful in it.

From the time they are in 9th grade (learners are) connecting with professionals from all different fields, visiting those workplaces and building networks that can lead to opportunities in the future. Those are opportunities families want for their kids[9].

Lillian Hsu, Principal

Some learners opt to undertake college course work online or through Community Colleges to gain credit in areas relevant to their emerging career or college goals, while entrepreneurship experiences such as business-plan competitions, prototyping and pop-ups enable learners to find out what it would take to launch and sustain their own business.

Motivation and engagement, both necessary precursors to deep learning and transfer, are activated when learners value and see the relevance of what they are learning and have a clear sense of purpose[10]. By connecting learning in and out of school, and the present challenges of education with future opportunities for work, Latitude helps learners to find the purpose and direction they need to work hard and be resilient.

A growth mindset, the belief in effort-based intelligence, is rooted in neuroscience that explains how the human brain literally grows as we learn[11]. Brain plasticity is the foundational concept for a range of learning strategies used at Latitude including multiple drafting and critique. Feedback is a staple of all classrooms, but in traditional schools the opportunities to act on feedback can be limited. At Latitude, in projects and extended learning opportunities, learners are expected to show the ways in which the feedback they have received has influenced their learning.

Design principles in action: Operational philosophy 49

In 'Workshop', learners work with peers and teachers to develop personalised learning plans and in 'Advisory' they receive coaching on their progress and can bring challenges and concerns to work through with their school 'family'. There is a strong focus in Latitude on nurturing positive relationships, which are explicitly designed to support learners' social and emotional growth and well-being, on the basis that these are fundamental to effective learning.

In such an academically robust and highly adventurous teaching and learning environment, Latitude's leaders know they must pay significant attention to the professional learning needs of their teachers.

Inspired by the 'thick symmetry' between the learning of students and teachers in High Tech High – what Hsu describes as HTH's 'secret sauce' – teachers take part in learning experiences that mirror those of their students. Through immersion in and by debriefing these learning experiences, teachers can apply their theoretical learning, to 'feel' metacognition and what it means to have a growth mindset[12] creating a 'double loop'[13] of experience and reflection that moves teaching practice forward in powerful professional learning

> *If you value students collaborating and communicating effectively, you create those structures that support teacher collaboration and communication[14].*

Design principle 7: Flexible/dynamic

The school should design and iterate different modes of teaching and learning to meet the evolving needs of learners and the wider world.

Launceston Big Picture, Tasmania, Australia

In 2016, Launceston City Campus was transformed into a Big Picture 'Demonstration School', the first stand-alone Big Picture school in Australia.

With just 150 students in years 9 to 12, Launceston is a close-knit community supporting learners to follow their passions through guided inquiry, and to explore diverse pathways through internships with organisations and entrepreneurs in the area.

Launceston is unlike other schools where there are teachers who organise learning in classrooms; there is a curriculum in which all learners must engage; and progression through learning that is governed by what comes next in the syllabus. In Launceston learners are centre stage and are supported by their teachers to engage in learning of their choice, at a pace that suits them and with mentors, their family, community groups and businesses as their guides[15].

This approach requires an entirely flexible curriculum, one that can adapt to the specific learning needs of individual learners and develop and shift over time as teachers' understanding of those learning needs grows and develops.

50   *Design principles in action: Operational philosophy*

Where, when, how and with whom learning takes place is tailored to the emerging needs of the learners in the school in that year and is remade each year as new learners join the Launceston community.

> *You're treated like an individual. It feels like I matter*[16].
>
> Jack, Year 12, Launceston Big Picture

Students develop learning plans and negotiate learning goals in collaboration with their teacher and their family, empowering them to take ownership of their learning throughout the year.

These personalised learning plans create a roadmap to help learners and their teachers together chart a course through the wide range of different modes of instruction and support available to them. As they follow their plan, learners are guided to note the learning goals that they achieve in five domains: quantitative, empirical, communication, social and personal.

Learners spend extended periods of time throughout the year on internships, connecting with their teachers remotely to discuss their progress. A technology-rich school, Launceston is well-resourced for learners to learn 'anytime, anywhere'.

During the COVID-19 pandemic, Launceston created opportunities for learners to participate in virtual 'speed career days' to learn about the inner workings of organisations across the State, and to make connections for internships once these could resume.

The development of learning plans continued, involving learners, teachers and families via their devices at home. Exhibitions of Learning also continued, with students showcasing projects and answering questions from a panel of community members and families via an online videoconferencing tool[17].

> *We continue to be impressed with the level of resilience and self-directed learning that our students have been able to demonstrate (through the pandemic).*
>
> Adrian Dean, Principal, Launceston Big Picture[18]

Design principle 8: Technology enhanced

Technology is used extensively and responsibly to liberate learning, amplify effective and diverse modalities, and to enable both personalisation and collaboration.

Technology enhanced: Individualised learning supported by AI

Chung Nam Samsung Academy, Seoul, South Korea

Chung Nam Samsung Academy (CNSA) in Seoul, South Korea serves 1050 students, 70% of whom are the children of Samsung employees. The school was opened in 2014 to provide a world-class education for Samsung's families

Design principles in action: Operational philosophy 51

because there was no education provision where they needed to live, in order to be close to where they work.

Competition for remaining places is fierce; 20% of students receive scholarships and come from deprived families in the Academy's neighbourhood, leaving just 10% of places available for local fee-paying families[19].

CNSA offers a university-style approach to learning designed to develop character, creativity and leadership. Programmes emphasise science and mathematics and most students join the school hoping to become part of the next generation of creative engineers "concerned with creating new technology, products and ideas that would bring harmony in our world[20]".

In the three years that they attend the Academy from ages 15 to 18, students follow learning programmes of their choosing from amongst a menu recommended to them via the Academy's online learning planner and based on their career aspirations. They call this 'moving study'; choosing between a range of five-hour units of lectures and tutorials offered on a rolling basis by specialist teachers, who make sure that core concepts and skills are in place to underpin students' independent learning.

Assessments are completed online on personal devices, and data analytics driven by AI provide real-time feedback to students about their achievements. The feedback indicates appropriate next steps and enables students to sign up for the next units they need to progress. These data are also available to teachers to inform the development of academic programmes and for pastoral support.

In addition to private study and instruction, students also collaborate to complete projects in industry-standard science, design and technology labs. Students learn to use state of the art technology including virtual and augmented reality, computer-aided design and 3D printing to complete science and engineering experiments and develop prototypes for new solutions to real world challenges.

Time spent in intensive team projects, rigorous academic programmes and independent online learning is balanced by a strong commitment to volunteering, which is actively promoted as a route to mental good health and happiness. Along with counselling provided by two full-time social workers and workshops about adolescent mental health for parents and teachers, volunteering forms part of a range of opportunities that specifically address the social and emotional development of students by "providing an environment where they fully develop into mature adults".

I think school should help people to be happy.

Principal, CNSA

Happiness amongst adolescents in South Korea is of particular significance. South Korea has the highest incidence of suicide by children of anywhere in the world, almost entirely associated with education and the pressure to enter one of a handful of high prestige universities[21]. At CNSA, no additional private tutoring is allowed, and students are encouraged to see music and sport as ways to alleviate stress and have fun as well as expanding their skill set.

52 *Design principles in action: Operational philosophy*

> **Design principle 9: Ecosystemic**
>
> Collaborative relationships are developed with many active partners in organising learning. Deep connections are made with the local community (and also to the global community through technology) to provide richer learning experiences and diverse pathways for learners.

Ecosystemic: Blurring the boundaries between school and the real world

Lumineer Academy, Melbourne, Australia[22]

When Susan Wu, one of Silicon Valley's Most Influential Women in Technology 2010, was looking for a school for her two-year-old in Melbourne, she struggled to find anywhere that met her exacting expectations. A successful tech entrepreneur, Wu wanted her child to have a learning experience that was creative and challenging, yes, but above all, one that was contemporary in its approach to teaching and learning, and future-focused in its curriculum.

> *If you look at the roots of our education system, it's in the industrial age, which valued mass conformity ... We can't predict the future, but we can make sure our kids are as prepared as possible for any version of the future ...*
>
> Susan Wu, 2018[23]

Designed by Susan Wu and a group of tech experts, educators and entrepreneurs, and co-founded with Sophie Fenton, Australian Teacher of the Year winner in 2013 Lumineer, which opened in January 2018, is a school that unashamedly sets out to reimagine education.[24]

Core to the Lumineer approach is the Luminaria, a model of learning designed by and for the school to "prepare children to understand, contribute to, and become courageous architects of our rapidly changing society".

The Luminaria model centres on STEM subjects – science, technology, engineering and mathematics – and explicitly integrates knowledge with skills, thinking with making, and scientific process with social and emotional growth, in a process Lumineers call multidisciplinary synthesis[25]. The focus is on whole child development in multiple dimensions: social, emotional, cognitive development and well-being, capacity for design and making.[26]

By balancing 'hard' subjects, like computer programming, with 'soft' skills like emotional intelligence and teamwork, learning at Lumineer models the interdisciplinarity of the real world and supports learners to grow the complex blend of knowledge, skills and attributes that is increasingly sought by employers.[27]

The commitment to real world learning is also reflected in the in-school learning environment the Lumineer team has designed. Students spend 70% of their time in studios – there are no traditional classrooms – engaged in hands-on

Design principles in action: Operational philosophy 53

making and building projects; tasks that bring subject matter and skills together and learning to life[28]. This emphasis on practical engagement springs from a belief that:

> *Learning, which is physically active, involves gathering information, thinking, problem solving, and attaining knowledge by participating or contributing has a significant advantage over passive approaches*[29].

Creating a complex learning environment that reflects the interdisciplinarity of the real world requires the school to develop partnerships with a wide range of organisations that can offer diverse learning experiences and authentic audiences for learners' ideas and solutions, for instance working with a wildlife non-profit organisation to design and build pouches for orphaned kangaroo joeys. As a consequence, assessment has a real-world feel, with feedback from authentic and expert audiences providing the necessary challenge and support.

Lumineer is also part of the local ecosystem; it is part of its neighbourhood. There is no playground at Lumineer, instead students are encouraged to take their breaks supervised in nearby public parks, modelling their connection to the community surrounding the school.

Teachers at Lumineer Academy are also deeply connected into a learning ecosystem. During a term-long Learning Exploration, Lumineer teachers work with a range of different activators and specialists in the fields they're studying.

Teachers have worked with nutritionists when crafting recipes, genetic research scientists when exploring the future of health tech, robotics engineers when building drones.

Their goal is to make the boundaries between the academy and the community as porous as possible.

In this chapter we have seen how different operational philosophies are applied in a range of contexts. From learning that makes the most of all that leading edge technology has to offer, including creating virtual realities, to learning that connects to the real world by blurring the boundaries between a school and its professional and geographic community, the operational philosophies of the founders, leaders and practitioners of these schools work to create alternative and powerful learning opportunities for the young people who attend them.

In the next chapter we turn our attention to the learners themselves; what they say and how they feel about their schools and their experiences in them.

Notes

1 Resmovits, Joy, Krishnakumar, Priya, and Welsh, Ben "California Must Find and Fix Its Worst Public Schools. Here's One Way to Start" *Los Angeles Times*, September 28, 2017 www.latimes.com/projects/la-me-edu-test-scores-2017-bottom-five/.

2 XQ Super Schools website "Latitude 37.8 High" Summer, 2019 https://assets.ctfassets.net/35eubtuv0bcm/1dEboz9bleBcSzJAPrlshy/b70d93fd1db589e06a9fece9609c4ebd/190815_School_PDFs_Latitude.pdf.

54 *Design principles in action: Operational philosophy*

3 In 2019 Larry Rosenstock, founder of High Tech High, was the Wise Prize Laureate recognising his extraordinary contribution to learning.

4 High Tech High website www.hightechhigh.org/.

5 Dumont, Hanna, Istance, David and Benavides, Francisco "The Nature of Learning: Using research to inspire practice" Practitioner Guide OECD CERI 2012 www.oecd.org/education/ceri/50300814.pdf.

6 Hattie, John A and Donohue, Gregory M "Learning Strategies: A synthesis and conceptual model" in *NPJ Science of Learning* online journal, August 10, 2016. www.nature.com/articles/npjscilearn201613

7 Ibid.

8 Dumont, Hanna, Istance, David and Benavides, Francisco "The Nature of Learning: Using research to inspire practice" Practitioner Guide OECD CERI 2012 www.oecd.org/education/ceri/50300814.pdf.

9 Oakland Charters, Medium "Building real world experiences at Latitude High" January 12, 2019 https://medium.com/oakland-charters/building-real-world-experiences-at-latitude-high-66d072aa9421.

10 Dumont, Hanna Istance, David and Benavides, Francisco "The Nature of Learning: Using research to inspire practice" Practitioner Guide OECD CERI 2012 www.oecd.org/education/ceri/50300814.pdf

11 Mindset Works "Decades of Scientific Research that Started a Growth Mindset Revolution" 2017 www.mindsetworks.com/science/.

12 Hsu, Lillian "Latitude High School: A Conversation with Lillian Hsu," Education Reimagined, March 19, 2019 https://education-reimagined.org/conversation-lillian-hsu/.

13 Instructional Design "Double Loop Learning (C. Argyris)" 2021 www.instructionaldesign.org/theories/double-loop/.

14 Oakland Charters, Medium "Building real world experiences at Latitude High" January 12, 2019 https://medium.com/oakland-charters/building-real-world-experiences-at-latitude-high-66d072aa9421.

15 Big Picture Learning "How It Works" www.bigpicture.org/apps/pages/index.jsp?uREC_ID=389353&type=d&pREC_ID=882356.

16 Launceston Big Picture School "What is LBPS?" YouTube November 14, 2018 www.youtube.com/watch?v=b4Mnk1OjkSM&feature=youtu.be.

17 Launceston Big Picture website "Principal's Report" https://lbps.education.tas.edu.au/newsletter/66328.

18 Ibid.

19 Yoon Min-sik "Samsung school accused of unfair admissions" *The Korea Herald*, October 21, 2014 www.koreaherald.com/view.php?ud=20141021000990.

20 Hashik Park "Principal's welcome to CNSA" CNSA website www.cnsa.hs.kr/hp wEng/about/welcome.

21 Ana Singh "The 'Scourge of South Korea': Stress and Suicide In Korean Society" in Berkeley Political Review, October 31, 2017 https://bpr.berkeley.edu/2017/10/31/the-scourge-of-south-korea-stress-and-suicide-in-korean-society/.

22 Note that Lumineer Academy has since been taken over by new leadership and renamed Newmark Primary. However, the core practice of engaging in real world problem solving for the surrounding community remains in evidence and with it the relevance of the ecosystemic design principle www.newmark.vic.edu.au/.

23 "Lumineer Academy Launching a New School for a New World" *The Australian*www.theaustralian.com.au/subscribe/news/1/?sourceCode=TAWEB_WRE170_a_GGL&dest=https%3A%2F%2Fwww.theaustralian.com.au%2Fnation%2Fnation%2Flumineer-academy-launching-a-new-school-for-a-new-world%2Fnews-story%2F1b30ea803a4d94f19ae14e1bd11bd325&memtype=anonymous&mode=premium.

Design principles in action: Operational philosophy 55

24 "Why this Tech Executive Says Her Plan to Disrupt Education is Different" *The New York Times* February 28, 2018 www.nytimes.com/2018/02/28/world/austra lia/school-tech-lumineer-academy-susan-wu.html.
25 Amanda Tawhai "Luminaria Educational Model" hundred 2021 https://hundred. org/en/innovations/luminaria-educational-model.
26 Ibid.
27 "Why this Tech Executive Says Her Plan to Disrupt Education is Different" *The New York Times* February 28, 2018 www.nytimes.com/2018/02/28/world/austra lia/school-tech-lumineer-academy-susan-wu.html.
28 Ibid.
29 Amanda Tawhai "Luminaria Educational Model" *hundrED* 2021 https://hundred. org/en/innovations/luminaria-educational-model.

6 Design principles in action
Learner experience

This chapter explores the design principles around the learner experience that we found in the analysis of the organisations surveyed. The principles are shown in Figure 6.1.

Schools may set out to operationalise their values authentically, but a *design principle* will always be highly attentive to the user experience. So it seems entirely appropriate – necessary even – to ask: What is it like to be on the receiving end? What do learners in fact experience in these schools? And how does that experience differ from their experience of more traditional schools, where they have had these?

In this chapter, we hear from learners directly about the effect of each design principle in this cluster on their sense of self, their confidence and self-efficacy and, of course, their motivation and capacity to learn. Learners' experience is the organiser in this chapter. Note that some of the learners' testimony is in translation.

> ### Design principle 10: Personalised
>
> The learner's experience relates to her personal needs, passions, development and purposes. These are at the centre: not the institution, the teacher, or external bodies of knowledge.

> *At Liger, I fell in love with marine biology. Last year, I created my own year-long project called Artificial Reef in Cambodia to provide a habitat for marine ecosystems, establish an anti-trawling reef, restore marine species populations, and increase the local knowledge of the marine environment. We have designed two types of artificial reefs and one of the designs was deployed off the island of Koh Seh Kep. I am very honored and proud to have the ability to make changes happen.*
>
> Soliday, age 18[1]

Liger Academy, one of the schools identified in Chapter 1, prioritises real world and purposeful learning through immersion in complex projects – here Artificial Reef – as part of their mission to educate and grow the next generation of Cambodia's leaders.

DOI: 10.4324/9781003244172-6

Design principles in action: Learner experience 57

This is just one of the ways that Liger personalises learning; in projects far beyond the scope of traditional school subjects, where learners can explore new areas of interest and contribute in unique ways that tap into what motivates and inspires them: they can fall in love with learning. Here's Vuthy, another Liger student, equally passionate, knowledgeable and skilled in a completely different area from Soliday.

> *Technology can help a lot of people and I felt satisfied when our tech support exploration was able to help other organisations in Cambodia. When I am not in class, I love to work on my computer coding, making websites or designing apps. I wouldn't know who I am and I wouldn't have found my passion without Liger.*
>
> Vuthy, age 18[2]

The opportunity to explore different kinds of work and career options is critical and many of the schools we have profiled prioritise time outside of school and in work placements of various kinds as part of the learner experience. Crosstown High School in Memphis, Tennessee, USA takes up two floors of the Crosstown Concourse, a city centre regeneration project housing a wide range of businesses in hospitality, healthcare, retail and financial services.

> *Being exposed to all the different jobs that are available here helps you think about what you might be interested in and want to do when you're older. It's better than being thrown out there and not knowing what you want to do.*
>
> Lauren, Year 8[3]

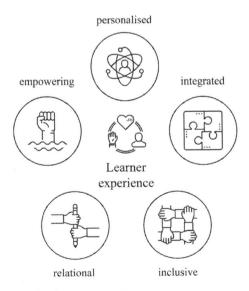

Figure 6.1 Design principles: learner experience

58 *Design principles in action: Learner experience*

Building enterprise skills in school and having an optimistic mindset about work are two of the four key factors known to increase young people's chance of finding meaningful work in an increasingly competitive and rapidly changing jobs market.[4]

Sometimes personalisation is about fitting learning around passions and interests that learners are already pursuing. Ylia is a student with Te Kura, a correspondence school in New Zealand that provides blended learning experiences for learners not in mainstream education.

> *It's focused on you as an individual, your weaknesses, your strengths, your interests. These are what your teachers and learning advisors figure out and they help you to arrange your education in a way that fits these best. It means I can base my education around what I want to do with my life and what I want to achieve, the projects and hobbies that I have. Te Kura has given me some epic opportunities and awesome support. The teachers and learning advisors are genuinely interested in your success as a student.*
>
> Ylia, Te Kura student[5]

Many traditional schools offer some degree of personalisation – some to a considerable extent. However, for the most part learning is personalised at the margins, in enrichment classes for instance, or in the arts. The reason we so rarely find personalised learning in core subjects is linked to standardised assessment. It stands to reason that a requirement to succeed in standardised tests militates against a truly personalised learning experience.

A distinguishing feature of a FutureSchool is a radical approach to assessment – personalised to the learner and fit for purpose to the task. Resisting the temptation to "teach to the test"[6] is just one of the ways in which leaders of these schools show courage and conviction.

Here's Ruby again, recent graduate from Green School in Bali, Indonesia, another of the schools profiled in Chapter 1.

> *Every single assessment task is formatted in a way that enables a student to choose how they want to show their own learning. If you're an introvert you could do it in a silent way – perhaps write a story, if you're good at creative writing. If you're interested in communications, you can host an assembly and educate the whole school community. Instead of just putting students all in the same box and assuming that will suit, students can learn in the ways that suit them, suit their own needs. It's so easy to create an environment where students feel empowered to use their own voice, where there are no restrictions as to how you can show what you're learning[7].*

Exciting as this approach to assessment is, it's easy to understand how it might feel risky in a traditional school. Interestingly, employers in increasing numbers are losing faith in standardised testing and are variously relying on interviews and extended inductions, or devising their own tests, to find the new hires they need for the future of their business[8].

> **Design principle 11: Integrated**
>
> The learner experiences meaning through learning that transcends siloes, building relevant connections within and between disciplines. This is about utilising many approaches: disciplinary; intra-disciplinary; cross-disciplinary.

When we look at schools pursuing integration, the feature we most frequently notice is a focus on real-world and project-based learning. In learning like this, subjects are blended, not discrete; science and literacy, for instance, are seen as inextricably linked and, more interestingly, educators understand that being better with language helps you to be a better scientist and vice versa. In their groundbreaking study of the role of metacognition in science education, stimulated by supporting students to study and solve real-world scientific puzzles and problems, researchers at King's College London found that improvements in science grades were matched by improvements in literacy outcomes[9].

Learning that integrates curriculum helps learners to make new and illuminating connections and, crucially, to stick with things long enough to understand them in depth.

> *Honestly, school wasn't going well for me. I was struggling in most of my classes. I learn by seeing things and by interacting with things. Now that we have this programme (Sci-gebra: integrating science with algebra) it helps us to get deeper into this stuff and learn things and really understand them, instead of a teacher just telling us to read a book.*
>
> Joshua, Year 9 student, Albemarle High School[10]

The combination of a sustained focus on an integrated project with real-world connections creates opportunities for future schools to make the learning experience feel relevant for and connected to young people's lives. Since Dewey, educators have understood the links between relevance and motivation to learn, and yet in traditional schools, the discrete focus on individual unrelated (and often unrelatable) subjects and the abstraction of classrooms from the outside 'real' world, leaves students "craving experiences that will broaden their often restricted understanding of the role of education in their lives"[11]. Others go further:

> *a thorough understanding of student motivation and the contextual effects that influence motivation is essential towards transforming schools from perceived intellectual prisons, devoid of relevance and personal meaning, to environments that support exploration, learning, and creativity among all students[12].*

Here's Ruby again, from Green School in Bali, Indonesia, explaining how she experienced a sustained, real-world project and what she learned that felt relevant to her.

60 *Design principles in action: Learner experience*

For six weeks straight, you work with nine other students and you design a project – something that you genuinely want to learn. We went to the 2017 UN climate change summit in Bonn, Germany and we spent six weeks planning what exactly we wanted to do there and what messages we wanted to bring. We wrote a play which we presented at various events. We learned project management, writing, team skills, communication and presentation. I learned a lot about collaborating in the real world, how frustrating it can be and how to be more tolerant and accepting.

Ruby, Green School[13]

Learning like this can be hard to evaluate using traditional approaches and, as we have seen, some schools are developing new forms of assessment to rise to the challenge. Those offering project-based learning experiences often use critique, an ipsative assessment method useful in situations where learners iterate and make multiple drafts during their projects, each of which is an improvement on the last.

Here's Kate from NuVu Innovation School in Cambridge, Massachusetts, USA. At NuVu, students collaborate in multidisciplinary studios using a design process to solve real world challenges; learning robotics, coding, fabrication, electronics and other technological skills. Projects are evaluated in critique by teachers, industry experts and end users providing detailed and specific feedback.

The critique process is definitely something that requires adjustment. When you're a creative person with big ideas it's really hard to separate those out from yourself. So it's very common for students to get defensive and to dismiss critiques just because it's so hard to put yourself out there. I've had critiques that have gone well and some that have made my eyes water. But I know these people are here to help me; these people are my family at NuVu.

Kate, 18, NuVu[14]

Design principle 12: Inclusive

The culture is experienced as respectful and welcoming.

When I come in in the morning the first thing we do is talk about what's happening at home and in my community. The teacher is trying to understand who I am and my values as a person.

Salma, Year 8 student[15]

The idea that teachers can and must 'know' learners to help them to be successful learners is a common theme. Educators achieve this through a variety of practices including coaching and mentoring.

One of the most frequently occurring and successful practices is known as advisory. In advisory, learners meet in small groups with one or two learning

Design principles in action: Learner experience 61

advisors, who encourage and support them to share challenges and successes and help them to navigate a course through their learning.

> *Advisory is my favorite part of the day. It's like your small home within the school. You're not just a number, you're not anonymous. School can be really hard for some of our students. We know them, we know their family, we know the community they come from. And because we know them deeply, we are able to approach students both personally and academically with a sense of respect and love and care*[16].

This is Joi Ward speaking. Joi is the social-emotional learning lead at Latitude High School, an XQ Super School[17] in Oakland California, which opened in 2018. However, Joi could equally be speaking from any number of the schools we have featured. In fact, advisory appears in the design for Latitude High partly because the school's co-founders and leaders are both alumni of High Tech High[18], one of the most successful and influential school models in the world,[19] where advisory is a key strategy for supporting learners to feel a sense of community and belonging, critical for the development of positive learning relationships.

Most traditional schools work hard to make learners feel welcome and included. Where the schools we have featured differ is in their determination to see diversity as an asset, and to design learning environments where differences of experience and perspectives are positive advantages, meaning learners from a wide range of backgrounds and cultures can come together and feel they belong and have value.

Liliana transferred in Year 9 from a traditional school where she felt "like an outsider" to USC Hybrid High School in Los Angeles, California, USA, where blended learning creates a college-style learning environment that prepares learners from diverse backgrounds for university[20].

> *When I came over here, I started being more proud of my culture. It's easier to relate when there's a lot of people like you. At the same time, it's also dope when there's diversity. I guess it just needs to be equally balanced. When you're a teen-ager you feel like an outsider already, even in just the slightest way. Here, I don't really feel like an outsider. I feel a lot more comfortable. When you have that sense where people care for you and for your success, it's better. I feel safe and nurtured. I think it's unique because a lot of us come from low-income families, and a lot of us are minorities, too.*
>
> Lilliana, Year 10 student[21]

Design principle 13: Relational

Individuals are known, good relationships are the basis for deep learning. Collaboration is the norm.

62   *Design principles in action: Learner experience*

What the science of learning and development tells us is that we need to create learning environments, which allow for strong, long-term relationships for children to become attached to school and to the adults and other children in it.

Prof. Linda Darling Hammond[22]

Relationships that create a sense of trust and safety are linked to agency; they are critical where the learning environment requires learners to take risks and responsibility for their own learning.

If I'm comfortable around them then I'm confident around them and it's easier to ask questions.

Cassidy, Year 8 student[23]

Sometimes I don't get along with the teacher and I'm like I can't do it, so I'm not going to do it. But when I like the teacher, I really want to do their work. I'll be like, I can learn this.

Aidan, Year 8 student[24]

Cassidy and Aidan connect their personal relationship with and trust in their teachers with confidence and motivation to learn. In the schools we have featured this connection is well understood, and respect and trust are actively pursued through the curriculum, for instance in programmes like those in School 21, UK and Riverside School in India, highlighted in Chapter 4, which explicitly explore diversity and identity and their role in building a better future.

XP school in Doncaster UK, is a future school, part of the expeditionary learning movement inspired by Ron Berger in the USA. Expeditionary learning centres on growing learners' curiosity and courage to learn through adventures and projects that take them outside their comfort zone, and often outside school.

To build the trust and confidence that learners need to feel safe to take risks, XP school starts with a literal expedition; learners and teachers spend a week away from home and school on a challenging adventure. During the expedition, learners find their 'crew', the teachers and friends who will support and challenge them throughout their time at XP.

For 45 minutes every morning learners work together in small groups that are formed in the first year they join the school. Crew is the unit in the school community that offers both support and challenge; where success is celebrated, and problems are understood and solved. Critically every member of a crew is responsible for the success and well-being of every other member:

We talk about being crew not passengers, and about getting everyone up the mountain. If a crew leaves anyone behind, we have failed.

Gwyn Ap Harri, Chief Executive, XP School[25]

Design principles in action: Learner experience 63

For me crew means to be part of a team, that we're all in the same boat, all on the same page, and if someone falls behind it's our responsibility to make sure they're on the same level as us.

Grace, XP student[26]

This sense of community and collective responsibility for everyone's success runs counter to a more familiar, individualised and somewhat competitive culture where learners are encouraged to "work hard" to get the grades they need for later success and reward.

The costs of this kind of learning experience can be high for learners. In a 2018 study by a children's charity in the UK, nearly half of all twelve-year-olds and 70% of sixteen-year-olds reported feeling sad or anxious at least once a week[27].

Schools do not do enough to address the growing mental health crisis among teens. We waste away our health education classes without learning valuable tools to deal with depression and anxiety. We need help with the real mental health challenges we face daily, often perpetuated within schools themselves[28].

Robert, 17, Indiana

The need for crew has never been more acute and educators in future schools are intentional and determined to be part of the solution for the learners they work with.

The trust with the teacher came when she kept on coming back. She never gave up on us. She kept on pushing us. She wouldn't stop − she wouldn't stop talking to us.

Bilikis, Year 11 student[29]

Design principle 14: Empowering

Learner agency (or self-direction) is developed, providing opportunities for learners to take increasing responsibility and ownership over their learning.

When students are agents in their learning, that is, when they play an active role in deciding what and how they will learn, they tend to show greater motivation to learn and are more likely to define objectives for their learning. These students are also more likely to have 'learned how to learn' − an invaluable skill that they can and will use throughout their lives.

Student Agency for 2030 OECD[30]

An explicit focus on empowerment with the goal of growing learner agency consistently features in these schools. Learners are actively encouraged to find, develop and use their voices.

64 *Design principles in action: Learner experience*

It is drilled into you from day 1 that you are important, that your voice is important. You are seen for who you are. You can go anywhere you want; do anything you want. I personally felt a strong sense of agency and intense passion for these issues. It's important to feel that sense as a young person that your voice matters, because you don't always see that in places around the world.

Ruby, Green School[31]

In School 21, in London, oracy is considered as important as numeracy and literacy and receives the same degree of explicit attention in school. Elsewhere we also see learners being encouraged and supported to grow their voice by presenting and debating their ideas and talking about their learning. At Wooranna Park in Victoria, Australia, learners present regularly as part of Enigma Missions, extended research projects in a focus area of the learner's choosing.

It starts out as an idea and flourishes into something that involves critical thinking and deep thinking. I study Area 51. It's an air force base in Nevada that was built in the space race period. This is my second year of research. I've presented six times. I've learned how to speak clearly and that also helped my confidence. Many students have asked me questions and pushed the boundaries of my project.

Aaron, Year 6, Wooranna Park Primary[32]

And here's Milo on how empowering he finds oracy learning at School 21.

What I like most about talking is that everybody's listening to you and you're like part of the world and you feel respected and important.

Milo, Year 3, School 21[33]

Learners feel empowered when they are encouraged to see themselves as agents of change; individuals with values, a sense of purpose, and the knowledge and skills to act on these.

I really feel like this school makes you feel like you can make change happen. You might not change the world – but you can change something.

Tiffany, High School student[34]

In traditional school you're thinking, this is the highest I can go, there are no further things I can do. When you take yourself outside of that box of traditional school you find there's endless possibility. Why do I have to wait until I'm an adult to take action and do this?

Abigail, High School student[35]

The schools we have featured empower learners by designing learning experiences where learners really do "make change happen" in the world. From running a charity at Riverside in Ahmedabad, India, to designing a better wheelchair at NuVu in the USA, these are schools that encourage learners to

Design principles in action: Learner experience 65

see themselves as a force for good in the world now – without the need to defer until adulthood.

I feel like I'm more of a person, someone who can take information and build something out of it and show people what I have to offer.
Year 10 student, Farm Roots Mini School[36]

Farm Roots is a 'mini school' in British Columbia, Canada; mini because learners aged 15 to 18 attend every other day – the remainder of their time is spent in traditional high school – to run a small, sustainable farm together. As well as hands-on experience in land management, learners gain credit in science, English, business and grow their leadership capabilities.

And finally, here's Ruby again on her sense of empowerment, developed through her learning experiences at Green School:

Real world challenges are important because when you step outside the bubble of Green School, it is a place of many obstacles and inequalities. You are hit by a sense of disempowerment and feeling that you're too small to make a change. It is about being seen and being acknowledged and valued as a learner. It's so important for self-esteem and confidence, so that when you step out into the world you feel you can make that change.
Ruby, Green School[37]

In this chapter on the design principles around the learner experience we have intentionally privileged learner voices over the researchers' or the providers'.

If we are concerned about inequity, or social exclusion, or growing levels of mental ill-health, it is imperative that the quality of the experience learners have is authentically considered, and that it is their perspectives that count.

It seems that if we want to grow generations with the qualities humanity now needs these schools may have hit on how to go about it.

Notes

1 Liger Academy "What Our Students Say" 2019 www.ligeracademy.org/impact/what-our-students-say/.
2 Ibid.
3 XQ America "XQ Awardee: Crosstown High" September 8, 2017 www.youtube.com/watch?v=JTwSK4TbufQ.
4 Foundation for Young Australians "The New Work Order Report Series Summary" July, 2017 www.fya.org.au/wp-content/uploads/2017/07/NWO_Report SeriesSummary-1.pdf.
5 Te Kura website "Learn with us about Te Kura" https://moetekura.cwp.govt.nz/learn-with-us/learn-with-us/about-te-kura/.
6 McGaw, Barry, Louden, William and Wyatt-Smith, Claire "NAPLAN Review Interim Report" November, 2019 www.education.vic.gov.au/Documents/about/p rograms/NAPLANreviewinterimreport_nov2019.pdf.
7 Interview with Valerie Hannon, June, 2020.

66 *Design principles in action: Learner experience*

8 Cale Guthrie Weissman "Why More Tech Companies Are Hiring People Without Degrees" *Fast Company*, April 3, 2017 www.fastcompany.com/3069259/why-more-tech-companies-are-hiring-people-without-degrees.

9 Adey P. And Shayer M. "Really Rising Standards Cognitive Intervention in Science Education" (London: Routledge 2014).

10 Mary Jo Madda "Albemarle County Schools' Journey from a Makerspace to a Maker District" EdSurge, May 2, 2016 www.edsurge.com/news/2016-05-02-albemarle-county-schools-journey-from-a-makerspace-to-a-maker-district.

11 Albrecht and Karabenick "Relevance for Learning and Motivation in Education" in *Journal of Experimental Education*, volume 86, Issue 1, 2018.

12 Gilman, R. and Anderman, E. "Motivation and Its Relevance to School Psychology: An Introduction to the Special Issue." *Journal of School Psychology*, 44, 325–329, 2006.

13 Interview with Valerie Hannon, June 2020.

14 NuVu "Kate's Story" YouTube, January 30, 2016 www.youtube.com/watch?v=Eui55R3NerA.

15 Edutopia "The Power of Relationships in Schools" January 14, 2019 www.edutopia.org/video/power-relationships-schools.

16 https://latitudehigh.org/about/.

17 The XQ prize in the USA was an open call to educators and communities to redesign the American High School for the 21st century. Prize-winning schools continue to be connected and supported in a network. https://xqsuperschool.org/about.

18 High Tech High website www.hightechhigh.org/.

19 Larry Rosenstock, founder of High Tech High, was in 2019 awarded the WISE (World Innovation Summit for Education) education laureate prize for his contributions to education globally www.youtube.com/watch?v=4rk6tp3rD0w.

20 https://rossier.usc.edu/usc-hybrid-high-school-will-open-in-the-heart-of-down town-l-a/.

21 Slapik, Magdalena "The Purpose of Education—According to Students" The Atlantic, October 1, 2017 www.theatlantic.com/education/archive/2017/10/the-purpose-of-education-according-to-students/541602/.

22 Edutopia "The Power of Relationships in Schools" January 14, 2019 www.edutopia.org/video/power-relationships-schools.

23 Edutopia "The Power of Relationships in Schools" YouTube, January 14, 2019 www.youtube.com/watch?v=kzvm1m8zq5g.

24 Ibid.

25 Interview with Valerie Hannon, July 2020.

26 XP School Website "We are Crew – Film" https://xpschool.org/we-are-crew-film/.

27 Hazell, Will "School Is 'the Main Cause of Stress' for Children" TES, February 5, 2018 www.tes.com/news/school-main-cause-stress-children.

28 McKormick, Kim R. "Young People Tell Us What Education Means to Them & 7 Ways to Improve It", IYF, August 12, 2019 www.iyfnet.org/blog/young-people-tell-us-what-education-means-to-them-7-ways-improve-it.

29 A New Direction "Beneath the Hood" www.anewdirection.org.uk/resources/creative-partnerships-resource-archive/films/beneath-the-hood.

30 OECD "Student Agency for 2030: Conceptual Learning Framework" OECD, 2019 www.oecd.org/education/2030-project/teaching-and-learning/learning/student-agency/Student_Agency_for_2030_concept_note.pdf.

31 Interview with Valerie Hannon, July 2020.

32 Edutopia "Passion-driven Research Projects" YouTube, August 2, 2019 www.youtube.com/watch?v=uHcZlBPD00M&t=3s.

33 Edutopia "Oracy in the Classroom: Strategies for Effective Talk" YouTube, September 20, 2016 www.school21.org.uk/.

Design principles in action: Learner experience 67

34 Coalition of Essential Schools "Building 21st Century Schools" YouTube accessed via http://essentialschools.org/about-ces/.
35 Education Reimagined "Learner Centred Education – What Makes it Possible?" https://education-reimagined.org/.
36 Delta Learns "Who Would Like Farm Roots Mini School?" 2016 https://vimeo.com/149243240.
37 Interview with Valerie Hannon, July 2020.

7 Can schools save us?

Emerging archetypes

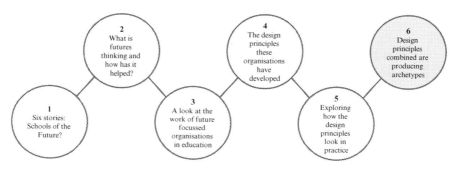

Figure 7.1 Step six

As the design principles for future schools became clearer, and as we reviewed the database of schools that were employing them, we started to notice clusters of schools emerging, which could be viewed as a set of *archetypes*. An archetype is a model or a particularly powerful example of a type, or paradigm.

There is an echo here of the approach taken by Howard Gardner in his seminal book, *5 Minds for the Future*[1]. He wasn't suggesting that the types of minds he was outlining there were mutually exclusive – on the contrary. The "5 Minds for the Future" that Gardner suggests identify capacities that he proposes each person should aim to develop. While no one person will be able to develop them all in equal measure, he argues we should aim to develop aspects of them all for the balance of mind needed for the future. Gardner was drawing attention to some dominant features, which were relevant in particular contexts. So too with this approach to future schools. No school is about just one thing.

In Chapter 1, we described the work of six schools we suggested could be seen as "six schools for the future". They were singled out not just because they were future-focused, nor only because they employed the design principles; but because they were also representative of increasing numbers of schools that are assembling their design principles to address a particularly pressing challenge of human existence at this juncture in history.

DOI: 10.4324/9781003244172-7

Can schools save us? 69

These archetypes create configurations of the design principles, around an overarching purpose creating a particularly powerful model. Again, we stress: no school is about only one thing. But these archetypes display – in their rearrangement of the basic building blocks of schooling (people, time, technology, place, partnerships) – fascinating possibilities of schools reconfigured for the future.

Archetypes: Powerful models of future schools

We discerned six such archetypes focused on distinctive future-focused missions. Of course, there may very well be more. The archetypes emerging from the data set were:

1 Schools emphasising our *environmental thriving*
2 Schools devoted to *growing ethical leadership*
3 Schools focused on *building our technological future*
4 Schools committed to enabling their learners to *navigate the fast-changing world of work and employment*
5 Schools that *grow entrepreneurs and changemakers*
6 Schools that give particular emphasis to nurturing a *sense of identity* in their learners.

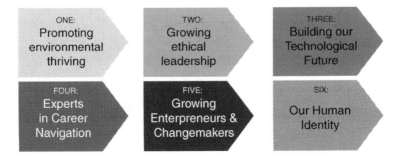

Figure 7.2 Six archetypes for the future?

Archetype 1: Promoting environmental thriving

The Green School (see p. 2 in Chapter 1) is representative of schools giving primacy to the idea that *we have no future unless every child becomes environmentally literate, passionate and active*. This is a fast-expanding category: worldwide examples include the Academy for Global Citizenship in the US; Spark Lynedoch, South Africa; The Muse School, California; Forest Schools; and many others.

As the climate crisis takes on ever more urgency, and global leadership appears inadequate to the task of addressing it, there is a hunger amongst young people to engage directly with this issue in an informed way, and not just await some dystopian future over which they have no control. On every continent,

70 *Can schools save us?*

aspects of the emergency are already with us; be it raging bushfires, floods, or extreme weather events. With every year we appear to pass another landmark: the hottest, the wettest, severest floods, most melting polar ice, most extinct species. And indeed, the interrelationship between humans' distorted relationship with the natural world reveals itself in seemingly unrelated phenomena. The evidence now appears clear that the coronaviruses are zoonotic[2]. They leap from wild animals to humans because of our careless interference with wild animals. Pandemics can arise from environmental ignorance.

Thus it was that in 2019 (pre-COVID) students took to the streets in their millions, striking from school, to protest this looming destruction of their futures – and also to demand that the issue became more central to their own learning and their capacity to respond to it.

It is therefore no surprise that educators and concerned parents are turning to consider what kind of education can be designed to help young people shape a viable future for the planet. In assembling combinations of the design principles, they have found a way to do it.

Archetype 2: Growing ethical leadership

The Liger Leadership Academy (LLA) (see p. 3 in Chapter 1) is archetypal of schools giving primacy to the notion that *the future demands new kinds of leadership: ethical, democratised*. This is a fast-expanding field. The United World Colleges, Future Nation Schools Africa, Mary L. Booker Leadership Academy, Nova Pioneer School … and many others. There seems to be a felt need to address the leadership deficit in this world of ours. The way in which the COVID pandemic played out globally threw into sharp relief how critical wise, competent leadership was to limiting the damage and achieving the best outcomes possible. What was valued was transparency – building trust, consistency, listening, being credible, and making sense of events for others. Jeff Holte (LLA's Director of Education) referred to that as the "ability to join the dots".

Of course, there have been kinds of leadership-focused schools for centuries. One such would be Eton College: it produced 20 prime ministers of the UK, five of them since World War II. But this is a form of leadership development based on privilege, entitlement, wealth, gender and class. Schools redesigned for the future are not replicating this model.

Firstly, it is held that great leadership can come from anywhere: it is not a matter of birth or position. Jeff Holte points to the nature of the leadership competencies, and how they can be acquired. Second, it is a matter of leader*ship* – not just individual leaders. Learning how to collaborate effectively in building vision, and how to implement it is a critical part of the competency set.

Again, it is literally vital to our futures that we produce leadership of a quite different calibre to that which prevails in the world today. These archetypal schools make it their central mission.

Can schools save us? 71

Archetype 3: Building our technological future

In the future (barring utter catastrophes) the pre-eminence of technologies – not just digital, but also convergences of technologies such as material sciences, blockchain, nanotechnology and biotechnology[3] – will create the most extraordinary opportunities as well as profound (even existential) challenges. This is beyond anything yet witnessed or even imagined by humanity.

We are seeing[4]:

- The construction of a planet-wide electronic communications grid, connecting the thoughts of billions of people at ever faster speeds, and linking them to exponentially expanding volumes of information and data.
- Webs of sensors being embedded ubiquitously across the world, such that the Internet of Things and 'the age of surveillance' are here[5].
- The development of increasingly intelligent devices and robots.

Evidence of profound change is already around us: ubiquitous, mobile super-computing, sophisticated robots, self-driving cars, neuro-technological brain enhancements, brain-computer interfaces (BCIs) and genetic editing. The question confronting us is: can the next generations ensure that technologies are created and deployed towards the thriving of humans and the planet?[6]

In the Kosen Schools (see p. 5 in Chapter 1), and schools such as Chung Nam Samsung Academy, Wooranna Park and many others, we found groups of schools that take as a guiding mission the idea that we need to create young people who are not just consumers, victims or objects of technology; but rather combine technological confidence and competence with the value frame that serves humanity. Indeed, Kosen schools set out to cultivate the next generation of what they called 'social doctors'[7] – creative engineers with strong academic and practical knowledge who could diagnose and solve issues in societies. The evolution of this type of school may be a fundamental part of our overall quest to thrive.

Archetype 4: Navigating the new landscape of work

One of the long-established functions of schools has been to prepare young people to become economically independent, and also contribute to the economy of their society. If asked, perhaps most young people would say that the key thing they wanted from their school was to enable them to make a living. So this is about *learning* a living. As the world of work has changed ever faster, the preparedness to continue to learn, to adapt to new conditions has become central. This idea of course has only been accentuated by the economic turmoil wrought by the pandemic. Employment prospects will be impacted, possibly for a generation. And all this is taking place in a context where automation and the impact of AI on the labour market creates even more uncertainty and volatility[8]. This issue is especially pertinent for families

72　*Can schools save us?*

and communities in deprived communities, living in poverty, who have traditionally not been well-served by education systems.

But although it has been an explicit goal of education systems, classically they have not been all that good at it. Skills gaps, youth unemployment have been markers of the system throughout the latter part of the 20th century[9].

This archetype comprises schools that are particularly focused on the idea that the future labour market will be disrupted, and volatile; and that *to ensure their future prosperity, learners need to become career navigators*. Tri-County Early College (see p. 5 in Chapter 1) models one way to go about this. Schools in the Big Picture family across the world make internships a central part of their offer to introduce their learners to multiple models of a working life.

This is a very different proposition from the idea that schools exist to service economies. That notion – sometimes explicitly promoted by politicians – may be what has perhaps made educators a little wary of embracing a close relationship with the world of employment. But in our upcoming future, the learning/earning boundaries will be smudged. And if young people are to flourish, they need the competencies to navigate the new world of work, even as it morphs before our eyes post-COVID-19.

Archetype 5: Growing entrepreneurs and changemakers

We suggest that LearnLife (see p. 6 in Chapter 1) is representative of the numerous schools now addressing the challenge of growing the world's capacity to create and manage change and innovation. This rapidly growing field is becoming increasingly studied[10]. It includes schools like the Riverside School (Delhi) and the NuVu Studio touched on in previous chapters (see p. 62 in Chapter 6). Movements such as Ashoka[11] have been at the forefront of pressing for – in their words – *"everyone a changemaker: a world where all citizens are powerful and contribute to change in a positive ways"*.

Now this movement is percolating into schools, explicitly drawing upon design principles for learning that develops the entrepreneurial competencies, and the value frame that drives motivation to make change for the common good.

Archetype 6: Finding our human identity

It is suggested that Nga Tapuwae (see p. 9 in Chapter 1) is archetypal of schools whose foremost mission is to help young people develop and discover their human identity. Perhaps this final archetype, focused on identity, is one that readers will find the most surprising. Or possibly not, if they are familiar with the strand of educational thinking that held education was about finding out who you are[12]. Schools focusing on this are to be found in the most unlikely contexts – for example, the Moonshot Academy in Beijing[13].

Now as we face the challenges of the future, the notion of identity has become more complex, more nuanced and more central than ever before. Because identity is not necessarily a fixed 'thing': it's a quest and possibly a struggle. It is a quest because humans' identity comprises many aspects in play. Nor is emphasis on identity unproblematic. As Francis Fukuyama shows in his book *Identity*[14], demand for recognition of one's identity is a master concept that explains much of what is going on in world politics today. The universal recognition on which liberal democracy is based has been increasingly challenged by narrower forms of recognition based on nation, religion, sect, race, ethnicity, which have resulted in anti-immigrant populism, the upsurge of politicised Islam, and the emergence of white nationalism. Identity politics gets a bad rap. In the context of the future this is even more complex. Now with us: issues such as gender fluidity/reassignment; and virtual identities in digital space. For schools of the future, these will be profoundly important issues to address[15].

Schools to build a thriving future

The archetypes profiled above are not intended as models to be copied, but rather as inspiring illustrations of how future-focused schools are now intentionally addressing different aspects of the human condition. The argument is not that they are all getting it 'right': our ideas about what 'right' looks like need to evolve too. But they are making a sustained effort to use the best intelligences, knowledge bases and highest aspirations to design the new institutions our species and the planet needs. They are focused on the key challenges and opportunities of the future: on realising the future we want.

Shaping the future we want in an age of disruption

Disjunctive change is characterising almost every aspect of human life from economies, politics, work, transport, healthcare – and above all in the climate emergency. That unfolding crisis underpins many other related disruptions – from migration to pandemics. The COVID pandemic is the first of a likely succession of zoogenic healthcare emergencies caused by an egregious failure of environmental stewardship[16]. Yet a further indicator of the new phase into which humanity has entered is contestation around what constitutes truth or factual knowledge. At the same time, the rapid development of convergent technologies and the awakening of new sensibilities, taken together with new sources of power[17] offer the most astounding opportunities for humankind – if only we can grasp them. The challenge for too many education systems is that they have not recognised the implications of this new phase of human existence for their own purpose: and for what and how children learn.

However, if the gravity – and the potential – of the moment have not been grasped by systems, they certainly have by school innovators. Even where it is not fully spelled out, one can discern in the archetypes we have described a profound understanding of the potential – or rather the need – for schools to step up.

74 Can schools save us?

What is it to thrive in the transforming world?

School is the only mandated institution that nearly all citizens encounter. What do we need schools to do for us, our societies and the planet? In a previous work[18] we have argued that the job we need schools to do for us as a species is to enable us to learn to thrive in a transforming world. That is a long way from the old notions of 'success' that have governed how schools have come to look. Thriving has to happen at four utterly intertwined levels (see Figure 7.3).

Ultimately, we cannot thrive if our planet does not. Three phenomena imminently threaten the capacity of the earth to remain a congenial home for our species. These are climate crisis, resource depletion, and destruction of biodiversity. These three threats are distinct, but of course, interrelated. They must be in sharp focus when we set our purposes for learning both because of the weight of evidence concerning the imminence of irreversible disaster, but also the huge potential for young people to take different approaches to these challenges than previous generations. Only by placing these three crises at the heart of education can we translate fear and urgency into action.

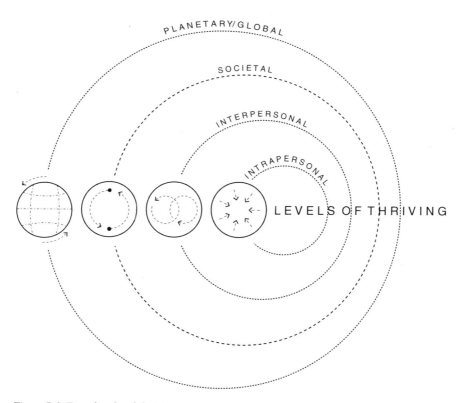

Figure 7.3 Four levels of thriving

The next level of thriving to which we must attend is that of thriving communities. Counter-intuitively, the evidence shows that it is not the wealth (by GDP) of a society that determines its overall well-being; but rather it is a question of how equitably its resources are distributed[19]. Of course, whilst work remains an important dimension of our societies, access to good jobs for all, equitably remunerated, is a key dimension of thriving communities. Thus equity – redefined and reconsidered – needs to be understood as a prerequisite for thriving societies. Schools can play a vital role in creating the conditions for that. But it requires a reconsideration of what is truly *valued;* and how those values are brought to life[20].

The third level of thriving is based on the fundamental truth about human beings: we are social animals. The quality of relationships with other people – family, friends, lovers, co-workers – is at the heart of whether life is satisfying or not. There is now strong longitudinal research evidence to support this intuitive sense. The Harvard Study of Adult Development[21] has tracked 724 men for over 75 years and studied the quality of their lives. Begun in 1938, it is the longest and most comprehensive study of its kind in the world. The director of the study summed up the findings of the research with refreshing simplicity:

> *The clearest message that we get from this 75-year study is this: Good relationships keep us happier and healthier. Period.*[22]

The capacity to make and sustain strong relationships is surely a learning goal – it should not just be left to chance, or family background. *It can be learned.*

And the final level of thriving is that of the interior life: the capacity of individuals to feel comfortable in their own skin, secure in the knowledge of who they are. The other pandemic of this age – that of mental ill-health – is less public and less dramatic; but it damages, and disrupts and causes immeasurable suffering.

The future schools profiled in this book understand the deep connections between these levels of thriving and ensure that they address each one of them in their learning designs. At the same time some archetypes are more profoundly aligned with particular levels: archetype 1 with thriving at the planetary level and archetype 6 with the intrapersonal for example. But there are no precise correspondences. The reality is messier. And that is the space for creativity: for leaders, educators and communities to consider their contexts, their community's needs: and ask *what is the job we need OUR school to do?*

And this brings us to the final chapter, in which we consider the leadership challenge all this presents.

Notes

1 Gardner, 2007. As a reminder, the five archetypal minds Gardner suggested were: The Disciplined Mind; The Synthesising Mind; The Creating Mind; The Respectful Mind; and The Ethical Mind. His purpose in proposing these ideas was to stimulate lifelong learning.

76 Can schools save us?

2 https://academic.oup.com/femspd/article/77/9/ftaa006/5739327.
3 Diamandis, 2020.
4 For discussions see Gore, 2013; Hannon and Peterson, 2021; Lovelock J., 2019.
5 Zuboff, 2019.
6 Zuboff, ibid.
7 www.jasso.go.jp/ryugaku/related/kouryu/2020/__icsFiles/afieldfile/2020/07/08/202007kosen.pdf.
8 Susskind, 2020.
9 Hannon V. et al., 2013.
10 See Zhao Y. 2012 and Wagner, 2012.
11 www.ashoka.org/en-gb/about-ashoka.
12 https://hundred.org/en/articles/why-is-identity-the-latest-focus-of-education#af1f1d92; and also https://esrc.ukri.org/news-events-and-publications/evidence-briefings/the-wellbeing-effect-of-education/.
13 https://en.moonshotacademy.cn/; see also Hall, 2016.
14 Fukuyama, 2018.
15 See Ball, 2019.
16 'How our abuse of nature makes pandemics like COVID more likely' in *New Scientist* 3/3/21 www.newscientist.com/article/mg24933240-800-how-our-abuse-of-nature-makes-pandemics-like-covid-19-more-likely/.
17 See Timms, 2018.
18 Hannon V. and Peterson A.K., 2021.
19 Wilkinson, 2009.
20 See Sandel, 2020 and Goodhart, 2020.
21 www.adultdevelopmentstudy.org/.
22 Robert Waldinger www.ted.com/talks/robert_waldinger_what_makes_a_good_life_lessons_from_the_longest_study_on_happiness/transcript?language=en.

References and further reading

Ball, Philip. *How to Grow a Human: Adventures in Who We Are and How We Are Made.* UK: HarperCollins, 2019.

Brey, Philip. "Human Enhancement and Personal Identity". In *New Waves in Philosophy of Technology*, edited by Jan Kyrre, Berg Olse, Evan Selinger, and Søren Riis, 169–185. Basingstoke, Hampshire; New York, NY: Palgrave-Macmillan, 2009.

Brynjolfsson, Erik and Andrew McAfee. *The Second Machine Age: Work, Progress, and Prosperity in a Time of Brilliant Technologies.* 1st edition. New York, London: W.W. Norton & Company, 2016.

Diamandis, Peter H. and Steven Kotler. *The Future Is Faster Than You Think: How Converging Technologies Are Transforming Business, Industries, and Our Lives.* New York: Simon & Schuster, 2020.

Frey, Carl Benedikt and Michael Osborne. "The future of employment: how susceptible are jobs to computerisation?" *Technological Forecasting and Social Change*, 114 (January 2017), 254–280. https://doi.org/10.1016/j.techfore.2016.08.019.

Fukuyama, Francis. *Identity: The Demand for Dignity and the Politics of Resentment.* London: Profile Books, 2018.

Gardner, Howard. *5 Minds for the Future.* Boston: Harvard Business Review Press, 2007.

Ghosh, Amitav. *The Great Derangement: Climate Change and the Unthinkable.* University of Chicago Press, 2016.

Goodhart, David. *Head Hand Heart.* London: Penguin Random House, 2020.

Gore, Al. *The Future: The Six Drivers of Global Change*. New York: Random House, 2013.

Hall, Ross and Ashoka Global Leadership Team. "Empowering young people to create a better world". Ashoka, August, 2016. https://issuu.com/ashokachangemakers/docs/empowering_young_people_to_create_a.

Hannon, Valerie, Sarah Gillinson, and Leonie Shanks. *Learning a Living: Radical Innovation in Education for Work*. 1st edition. London: Bloomsbury Academic, 2013.

Hannon, Valerie and Peterson, A.K. *Thrive: The Purpose of Schools in a Changing World*. Cambridge: Cambridge University Press, 2021.

Lovelock, James. *Novacene: The Coming Age of Hyper-Intelligence*. Harmondsworth: Penguin, 2019.

Sandel, Michael. *The Tyranny of Merit*. London: Allen Lane, 2020.

Susskind, Daniel. *A World Without Work: Technology, Automation and How We Should Respond*. London: Allen Lane, 2020.

Timms Henry and Heimans J., *New Power*. New York: Doubleday, 2018.

Wagner, Tony. *Creating Innovators: The Making of Young People Who Will Change the World*. New York: Atria Books, 2012.

Wilkinson R. and Pickett K., *The Spirit Level: Why Equality Is Better for Everyone*. Penguin Books, 2009.

World Economic Forum. "The Future of Jobs: Employment, Skills and Workforce Strategy for the Fourth Industrial Revolution". Global Challenge Insight Report. Geneva: World Economic Forum, January 2016. https://reports.weforum.org/future-of-jobs-2016/.

Zhao, Yong. *World Class Learners: Educating Creative and Entrepreneurial Students*. Corwin Press, 2012.

Zuboff, Shoshana. *The Age of Surveillance Capitalism: The Fight For a Human Future At the New Frontier of Power*. London: Profile Books, 2019.

8 The leadership challenge of a generation

The explorations conducted for this book have suggested a framework for addressing the challenge of how we should be creating schools that are fit for the future. We take the view that schools as institutions are *needed* to enable our species and our planet to thrive in fresh and significant ways. But they need to change in order to do so.

After our journey exploring the work of existing future-focused schools, we return full circle to reflecting on how futures thinking might be employed to help leaders rise to the challenge of their generation: using the historic opportunity a pandemic has presented to create schools fit for *all* learners in the unprecedented times we face. The need is for leaders who can undertake 'cathedral thinking': a far-reaching vision, a well-thought-out blueprint, and a shared commitment to long-term implementation. It is how Greta Thunberg frames the demands from the coming generations to those now in power. What does this look like when applied to education policy and practice, when systems have proved so resistant?

The focus on 'leaders' in the conventional sense here should not be taken to suggest that others do not have a hugely important role to play. The pressure from learners themselves, as their agency grows, may well prove a game changer. Through COVID-19, parents have had a closer look at the learning process and schools' offer to their children: they may well become a more proactive force. Business and civil society understand increasingly that education is everybody's business.

But the purpose of this chapter is to offer some perspectives, strategies and tools to the leaders charged with the responsibility for education's future. The design principles that have emerged from our analysis, and the experiences of those who have gone before, provide a rich palette for creating imaginative and bold visions of future schools. The time is right, the examples abound, and the design principles provide the tools for the work.

The pandemic's gifts: Insight

In discussing the pandemic's legacy thus far, we have focused on the more negative aspects – albeit noting that an enlarged appetite for change may have emerged. But there has been real learning[1]:

DOI: 10.4324/9781003244172-8

The leadership challenge of a generation 79

- Teachers can learn new roles and skills fast, and be highly adaptive
- The physical, person-to-person dimension is lost only at great cost
- That a strong sense of community focused on the school is an invaluable asset
- Features previously seen as secondary are actually of extreme importance (the relational and social; the safe custodial)
- That despite schools' poor record in achieving equity, nonetheless without them the alternative is worse
- Channels for acquiring knowledge and skills are now multiple; schools no longer have the monopoly – and this has opened up new possibilities for schools themselves.

Thoughtful system leaders – political or professional – need now to be considering how these insights can be combined with the work of the innovative, future-focused organisations and schools profiled here. But how?

Beyond pockets of brilliance

Many – though by no means all – of the examples of schools cited in this book that are intentionally orienting to be future-fit are operating outside of the public systems. Across the world numerous start-ups are appearing. A few are state-sponsored such as in Beijing and Qatar. School chains, utilising configurations of the design principles described earlier are multiplying: from the United World Colleges; Round Square; Whittle Schools and Studios; and micro-schools such as Agile Learning Centres, Quantum Camp, Acton Academy, and many more.

Since so many such schools are fee-paying or independent, they are available to elites: discerning parents who can see what is needed and afford to pay for it. A serious concern is that the advantaged will access future-facing schools whilst many schools in the public sector remain constrained by the old paradigm: partly because the *public will* has not yet been built to effect a shift; and partly because teachers are not trusted sufficiently to reorient in these directions. Too many state schools are stuck in the slow lane. So what can leaders do to bring their systems up to speed? If we want the opportunities they offer to be available to all learners, what is the way forward? In particular, what is the role of system leaders in creating the conditions in which school leaders – especially in the State sectors – can move in this direction and become a part of the new paradigm?

Gwyn ap Hari, the Principal and co-founder of XP schools in Doncaster UK (featured in Chapter 6) is an educator deeply embedded in the State sector in a deprived post-industrial area. He is insightful about the challenges innovators in the sector face:

> *It's a matter of will. I can understand how hard it is to move from one thing to another. But we have similar problems as well. We call it entropy. If you don't inject energy into a system, the people in that system will go towards whatever's*

80   *The leadership challenge of a generation*

easiest. What's the easiest thing to do? For a teacher, it's to rock up, talk at the kids for a bit, and then go home. But you've got to inject energy into the system, – create the structures. In this school, that's about creating the narrative arc, working with other teachers to get the benefit of cross-curricular expeditions. I can show all those things that we do; but that doesn't allow some people who feel stuck in where they are, to get to where they need to be.

From my perspective, I could say they are just excuses: you can do it, because we've done it. But it's hard. It's complicated. It's scary. Not many other people are doing it. So I do understand why people choose not to. But it is a choice[2].

Gwyn has done the hard yards, and his start-up within the State sector is now secure, growing, and influencing the local system in a myriad of ways.

What then can system leaders do to "inject energy into the system" and become active leaders of change, not bystanders? How can they release the energies and agency of school leaders? We offer the following six strategies, in the full knowledge of the political complexity of acting in this space: but convinced too of its urgency.

An agenda for leaders: Six strategies to consider

1. Build the public will for change

A major blockage to change is politicians' assumptions about what the public wants or will tolerate. But they have a role in creating a different culture of expectation – and the pandemic may help in that, since so much is being re-evaluated. We need new narratives of what education is for and what it can be. The diverse experiences of parents, educators and young people of the disruption of learning during the pandemic can be a springboard for the development of such narratives.

Leaders are looked to more and more to provide a sense of purpose and coherence through narrative; being able to tell a story about where we have come from, where we could be going, and what the milestones might be. The power of stories in mobilising energy and commitment, and in bringing together disparate resources into more powerful wholes, has always been particularly evident in education. The task of leadership includes being able to fire the imagination, as well as to generate and orchestrate the processes that can increase the range of what is possible. What often gives such leadership wider resonance and impact is its ability to project moral purpose, to make explicit and practical the basic commitments and intuitions that others have about what is of value. Building the public will for a better future requires strategy, insight and coordination. It entails understanding and talking with broad audiences, not just those who already agree. Often this is not (only) about data. It is also about storytelling, along the lines of *this is necessary and within reach*, and *we're at a juncture where we can get it right*.

What is the prevailing narrative about education? It is worth spelling it out. The features of the old story are easy to list – even though they are not made explicit too often, since naming them reveals their bankruptcy. We use that term deliberately because the underlying model is economistic.

Key features include:

- Education makes nations more prosperous because it increases growth (GDP)
- Education is the route to the best jobs
- Education is the route to social mobility
- Success in education is getting qualifications
- Subject-based academics are the qualifications that really matter
- Getting into university is a key success indicator; if you haven't got a degree, you are second class

It is interesting that economists[3] themselves are raising issues of the nature of *value/s* at this time. Of course, the concept lies at the heart of the discipline of economics; but a new breed of economists has begun to argue for a reassessment of the idea. Amongst the most eminent perhaps, Mark Carney (former Governor of the Bank of England) has examined how economic value and social values became blurred, how we went from living in a market economy to a market society. Everything has become commodified, and price is equated with value. Commodification is corroding; we have placed the things which in truth we need to value at profound risk. Carney sets out a framework for an economic and social renaissance in a post-COVID world, which embeds the values of sustainability, solidarity and responsibility into all decision-making. These values are currently notable by their absence.

The age of disruption we have entered is such that it is the duty of education leaders to understand its contours and implications. Constructing a new narrative and the means to communicate it are the necessary preconditions for achieving consensual deep change. That depends on building political will, the will of stakeholders, the public will and crucially the will of young people. The construction of a fresh public narrative (the story we tell ourselves about ourselves) is fundamental to any possibility of change in education, the change that is needed if today's learners are to thrive in a transforming world. This will build the platform to bypass or leapfrog institutional arrangements that hold on to the old grammar of schooling. It will enable the essential innovation in pedagogy, curriculum choice, assessment and culture. But it entails leaders becoming storytellers as never before: wherever they get the opportunity, opening up a different kind of conversation about schools' role in creating the future we want[4].

Are there any systems where leaders are moving in this direction? There are some encouraging signs. Recent political leadership shown in New Zealand may offer some indicators. In 2018 the newly elected Prime Minister Jacinda Ardern (whose subsequent leadership of the country during the COVID crisis

82 *The leadership challenge of a generation*

earned global recognition and praise) launched a "Big Conversation" about the future of education in the country, beginning with two large and highly inclusive "Summits on the Future":

> *We need your help. We don't simply want to impose our ideas about what might be best … We want you to help us shape the future, so all our lives are improved. I encourage you to come up with ideas and have your say. Help us to design the best education in the world*[5].

A series of changes is now underway in New Zealand (at time of writing, planned for implementation to start in 2022) in part as a result of the conversation about the future. These include a changed relationship between the Ministry and schools[6]; and curricular reviews that focus on relevance, identity and critical thinking. These are aligned indeed with the design principles for the future we have identified[7].

2. Enable a different professional debate

How might we encourage informed, systematic debate about the school design principles: what they mean; what they are based on; where is the research on how they are best implemented; and what are the practical implications? The set of principles laid out in this book have been synthesised from the work of some of the key future-focused organisations, in an iterative process with innovative practitioners. That does not make them comprehensive: no doubt others might arise in the debate. Probably, as discussed in previous chapters, the mix to be adopted will vary from context to context.

The design principles speak directly to the challenges and opportunities of the pandemic precisely because they originate from people and places committed to preparing young people for a future that anticipates, for instance, uncertainty and complexity as part of the day-to-day human experience.

But what is needed is the space and scaffolding to encourage learning communities (of whatever stripe) to engage seriously with design principles for future-focused learning, some of which they will have been working towards realising. Others will be confronting. A serious cause for optimism is the rise of professional learning communities and networks amongst teachers across schools to seize their professional development and growth. The interest in schools as learning organisations is an example of this.[8] How much more powerful would this be, were this to be systematically supported and explicitly futures-oriented?

As we argue elsewhere[9], a different kind of professional debate would mean that we:

- Place purpose and focus upfront, with the requirement really to debate what the goals are
- Acknowledge the complexity of educational goals and problems, not falling back on managerial linear planning techniques

The leadership challenge of a generation 83

- Emphasise the importance of involving and engaging the most important actors – the learners, their families and their communities
- Rely upon convened teams of empowered educators to explore, enquire, learn and implement together in a structured, disciplined way.

Leaders who become competent in these approaches are able to engage in future-focused innovation with real professional responsibility. We stress competency here, since these are learnable approaches in which leaders can demonstrate proficiency. However, a precondition for their effective deployment is a real shift in mindset: a move away from that of the service manager, to that of the social entrepreneur and changemaker.

An excellent example of this would be the journey undertaken in British Columbia, Canada in the last decade. As described by Sanford and Hopper[10], an already 'high-performing' system (on the old metrics) was nonetheless discontented with its fit with both its own values and the contours of the future. It wanted a framework to assess students' successes over time, and to provide teachers with the flexibility in curriculum design to address current world, real-life problems with their students. Key to the success of the transformation that is underway has been the interconnectedness of political leaders with the educators, school and district administrators and teachers, all bringing strengths to reshape the curriculum for more innovative educational practices and thinking. A different kind of ongoing dialogue has been created. It is one from which learners can only benefit.

3. Be leaders unafraid to lead

Within the public system, even the most innovative and forward-thinking principal frequently feels caged, constrained by bureaucratic or outdated regulations or assumptions. However inspiring their vision, 'the system' is often cited as the limiting, not the enabling factor. This is by no means a question of money. It is the principal reason why so many of the future schools springing up are start-ups outside the public system.

It is surely right that political leaders determine the overall direction of travel for a system: after all, it is fundamental to the nature of the State and should enjoy a democratic mandate. Their work – as we have argued above – is to build the public will for change and create the enabling conditions for transforming the system. This is what is underway in systems – already 'high performing' on the old – such as Finland, Singapore and New Zealand.

System leaders – the civil servants sometimes pejoratively termed 'bureaucrats' – have a particularly crucial role in offering real leadership. They need to enrich the ideas pool and evidence upon which politicians can rely. And they need an unbureaucratic mindset: more outward looking, curious, and open to new developments. Informed by design principles, they need to be more willing to consider different uses of time, space, people and technology. They need the kinds of mindsets that Kaser and Halbert describe in their study of leadership for transformation[11].

84 *The leadership challenge of a generation*

It has been observed[12] that we need not just innovative solutions, but *system innovation*. More fundamental innovation is needed in two situations: first, when a challenge is stuck and significant gains can no longer be achieved using the same system model. And secondly, when society faces a new, systemic challenge that existing systems were not designed to cope with. Both of these conditions obtain now, in relation to education systems. Moreover, innovation is not just about problem solution: it is also fundamental to the seizing of opportunity[13]. A systemic opportunity is never just a different way to achieve an existing goal: it makes new goals, and ways of life, possible. As we have argued, education systems should now be deeply engaged in the task of creating a new, thriving way of life.

4. Lead for innovation: Link R&D to real scale

R&D (Research and Development) in education is usually equated with the evolution of edtech. However, the urgent and under-resourced need is for an R&D system applied to the institution of schooling itself. In most education systems, there is an informal network of R&D (perhaps better described as D&R since it is often practice-led). Pioneering collective efforts to develop and scale forms of education innovation have been steadily growing in the last two decades. Amongst others, they include not-for-profits like Innovation Unit (UK and ANZ), Edutopia, Education Reimagined, Remake Learning; for-profit consultancies; and in some instances, state-backed initiatives (the New York City i-Zone, and the Finnish NAE Innovation and Development Centre).

A range of well-evidenced and developed methodologies now exists and is readily available to be deployed in the endeavour. They may not be standard in leadership development programs; but their use is growing and expertise becoming more widespread. They include methods like *Agile Leadership*[14] , *Spirals of Enquiry*[15] and *Human-Centred Design*[16]. What is needed now is system leaders to promote their use and enable implementation of the outcomes.

The issue is: how can we move from the relatively isolated exceptions represented by the instances profiled in this book, to these becoming the norm? Where is the theory of change that addresses this issue?

One individual who has developed such a theory is Christopher Pommerening, one of the founders of *LearnLife*, whom we met in Chapter 1. Pommerening is a reformed venture capitalist who has taken what he describes as a '180-degree turn' to become a social impact entrepreneur. He has no interest in merely seeding a single lab school of the future in one location – or indeed in many. Christopher is aiming at system change. His team is looking to empower 100m learners in the new paradigm; and believe they can achieve a tipping point in the next ten years. In that time, they are looking to work with educators who are innovators and early adopters. Beyond Barcelona, they are in advanced negotiations with the City of Hamburg to create a LearnLife Hub that will work in concert with the city's existing schools.

The leadership challenge of a generation   85

> *We think that if we build a learning ecosystem at a local level, it will have so much impact and inspiration power that it will eventually change the mindset of people – including government officials. We are just testing this in Spain, and now in Hamburg. We are about revolutionising school systems. There are so many beautiful projects out there, but they are all frustrated. Why? We think it is because the value proposition is to operate on a local or regional level. There are plenty of schools, say in Germany, that are lab schools; but they are parochial, looking at what is happening locally. We are completely international, aggregating the best thought leadership from across the world. We are working with 300 thought leaders from around the world, looking at a whole range of methodologies. You can then 'package that backwards' and make it relevant to a local system. We want to be 'venture builders', asking: what next after schools? We think the answer is Learning Hubs. But we must influence governments. For example in Barcelona: already the government has taken their inspirations from us and incorporated them into their architectural manual. In Hamburg plans are advanced. LearnLife has now been approached by entrepreneurs and 5 Government agencies – without our reaching out – who want to build Learning Hubs in 25 countries and 43 cities[17].*

A further interesting example is '4.0' in the US[18], which has been founded explicitly to develop leaders who are professionally equipped and courageous enough to found new schools for the future. They look for Fellows who are early-stage leaders and innovators with a passion for redesigning education.

Perhaps one solution to education systems' notorious inability to generate paradigm shift from within is for more of them to partner with not-for-profit entrepreneurial groups to address the challenge. Of course, this depends upon having built a public will for change – the first point made in this section. The alternative may be that the publicly funded schools, despite extraordinary efforts by some school leaders, continue with the glacial rate of progress.

5. Think ecosystems not systems

One of the future-focused design principles that emerged in our scan was to be ecosystemic as institutions; making better use of the sequestered learning assets of culture, sport, business, not-for-profits, media and community. But that principle needs to apply to school *systems* too. The front-loaded vision of education that emerged in the 19th century still haunts us. The schools, university and vocational systems in many contexts operate quite independently. One cannot think of future-fit schools without reassessing the entirety of the ecosystem into which they should fit. No vision of learning that is lifelong and deep can be realised without radically reconnecting institutional systems that currently act in silos.

In a study of 40 learning ecosystems worldwide, Luksha et al.[19] offer the following definition:

> *Learning ecosystems are interconnected relationships organising lifelong learning. They can also be described as intentional webs of relational learning which are*

86 *The leadership challenge of a generation*

dynamic, evolving, and enable greater diversity when fostering lifelong learning opportunities. They connect learners and community to develop individual and collective capacity. The purpose of learning ecosystems is to offer pathways for learners to actively co-create thrivable futures for people, places and our planet …

The shift from industrial education to ecosystemic learning requires a seismic shift in leadership. Ecosystem leadership is emerging as a potential pathway to unlearn, reimagine, and relearn how to both learn and lead together as we co-create life affirming futures together that work for all.

Put bluntly, if we are to thrive, education needs to be "everybody's business". Doncaster UK (where XP School is located) under the leadership of its visionary Chief Executive Damian Allen, is creating a Talent and Innovation Ecosystem, to draw in and exploit new providers, partners and innovation in order to transform the life chances of kids who have been under-served by the education system for generations. Helsinki has explicitly declared itself a learning ecosystem – a holistic learning environment[20].

Again, the pandemic has provided a powerful nudge: the challenge to the business models of many universities (based on overseas student fees) has led to many reconsidering their role and relationship with their domestic communities. Swinburne University in Australia was ahead of the game in this area. Well before the pandemic hit it decided to forge powerful linkages and frictionless exchange with their home school community. Tri-County Early College (profiled in Chapter 1) and The Met Big Picture School (Rhode Island) are examples of school-led efforts to position themselves as part of a seamless learning ecosystem with their local colleges. But this move should not be dependent upon individuated efforts, often straining to circumvent regulations (around funding particularly) that hinder this shift. It is a shift that is essential for a future-fit *system.*[21]

6. Utilise futures thinking

Finally, we revert to the question posed at the top of this chapter. In the aftermath of the COVID-19 pandemic, education leaders are struggling to manage the many challenges they face. These are:

- Economic – funding their systems in the face of the consequential financial challenges
- Social – addressing the even greater inequities that have arisen, together with new levels of mental health issues and, of course,
- Educational.

Almost every aspect of life seems set to change as a result of the 2020 crisis: how can leaders ensure that education too becomes adaptable to future conditions?

In Finland, the Parliament has a "Committee for the Future". All ministries prepare their own "Futures Reviews". The Finnish National Agency for Education runs a Future of Learning 2030 Barometer exercise, which relies on the techniques of futures thinking, including scenarios. Here system leaders are not bureaucrats, but active enablers of imaginative thinking and action. The 2018 curriculum reform process closely reflected the issues that arose through this barometer, especially changing roles of teachers and learners, crossing boundaries between school and society, and putting competencies at the heart of learning.

Similarly, Singapore has a Centre for Strategic Futures[22] (based in the prime minister's office), which maintains a network of practitioners of various ministry and agency foresight units, and international thought leaders. The aim of this work, again, is not prediction; but to develop a mindset and culture of future-orientation. Interestingly, the narrative developed around the policy changes that have emerged has been couched in simple and fresh language: 'Learn for Life'; 'Joy of Learning'; 'Teach Less, Learn More'. This is a long way from the familiar education arms-race narrative.

We believe that the intelligent use of futures thinking may help; as well, of course, as the application of knowledge about learning. Futures thinking can grow the ability to comprehend change. It can help to overcome fear and inspire hope. At a time when economic visions, belief systems and cultures are all up for grabs, there is a need to work out the contours of a future framed according to our values. That is why the tools and processes of futures thinking are so valuable – to leaders in particular.

We have drawn in this book on the work being pursued by a range of important futurist organisations across the world. The challenge is to make this work accessible and adoptable universally. 'Futures literacy' needs now to be an integral dimension of preparation for leadership – and there are processes and approaches that can equip leaders with the necessary knowledge, skills and values. This is about creating leaders who can navigate different time horizons with the goal of ensuring that our learning systems realise the new purposes: individual and collective thriving. As an illustration, two futures-thinking tools might be mentioned.

(a) The frame of three-horizon thinking

A device being utilised in a number of organisations – government and corporate[23] – may increasingly be useful in the context of education. It involves intentionally conceiving of the nature of the tasks ahead on three horizons.

In the graphic (Figure 8.1), horizon one recognises that leaders must focus on managing immediate recovery. It entails "necessary myopia"; but not without an eye to the longer term. Horizon two is the point of transitioning. Arguably, schools and systems will be in this space – a "zone of collision" – for some time. Change theorists believe this is the time of greatest innovation and disruption, when immediate dangers have receded, and where new thinking can emerge. But the key is to put in place arrangements fitted to the third horizon, where a new paradigm comes to be built, capturing the "future we want". But the idea is precisely *not* to put off that work: it needs to start now. The pockets of the future are already in existence.

88 *The leadership challenge of a generation*

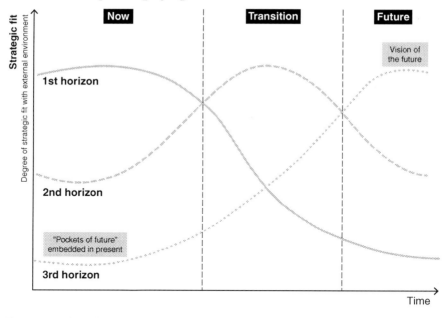

Figure 8.1 Three-horizon thinking

Using this device, leaders can encourage those they work with to keep in view, and work towards, the new; whilst they necessarily grapple with a tough immediate present.

(b) The scenarios frame

One approach to cathedral thinking, or the 'third horizon', is for leaders to examine and explore scenarios. In Chapter 2 we introduced the idea of the "zone of plausibility" and noted that the pandemic had widened this considerably. It is an aspect of "*the virus rewriting our imaginations*". Exploring scenarios is a useful method for navigating the zone of plausibility, and working towards a preferred future. The purpose of working with scenarios is not to predict the future. Rather, it is to imagine future contexts that could plausibly arise, and use them to inform strategic decisions about how to act in order to bring about the future that is preferred. They can only come alive when considered against a particular context. The point is to create a dialogue. That can be done by looking at each scenario and assessing its likelihood; considering the threats and opportunities each one presents; asking what new options present themselves.

The work of the OECD is by far the most developed in using this technique[24]. It has suggested that working with foresight scenarios has a number of objectives:

The leadership challenge of a generation   89

- Anticipation: identifying what's changing; considering developments that do not seem intuitively relevant, or likely
- Policy innovation: helping to reveal options for action that make sense in new circumstances
- Future-proofing: stress-testing existing plans, strategies, or policies

What then might be some plausible scenarios for the education landscape post-COVID-19? The OECD work sets out four:

Scenario one: Schooling extended

In this scenario, participation in schooling continues to expand. More individualised learning is supported by increased use of technology. However, the structures and processes of schooling remain unchanged.

- Education system monopolies remain: schools are key in socialisation, credentialling and care.
- International collaboration and better use of technology power more personalised teaching and learning practices.
- The profession of 'teaching' remains fundamentally the same.

Scenario two: Education outsourced

In this scenario, traditional schooling breaks down as society becomes more directly involved in educating its citizens.

- Self-reliant 'clients' look for more flexible services.
- Schooling systems become one amongst other players in a wider education market, without boundaries.
- There is a diversity of 'teaching' roles operating within and outside schools.

Scenario three: Schools as Learning Hubs

Schools remain, but diversity and experimentation become the norm. Schools become ecosystemic, connecting communities.

- Strong focus on local decisions. Schools are self-organising units in diverse partnerships.
- Flexible school attendance arrangements enable greater personalisation and community involvement.

90 *The leadership challenge of a generation*

- Professional teachers become choreographers of wider networks of teaching expertise and knowledge.

Scenario four: Learn-as-you-go

Education takes place everywhere, any time. Distinctions between formal and informal learning are no longer valid.

- The dismantling of schooling as a social institution. The traditional goals and functions of schooling are superseded by technology.
- Individuals become 'prosumers' – both consuming and producing knowledge and skills. Communities of practice become central.
- Governance of data and digital technologies becomes key.

It is important to stress that the purpose in exploring scenarios is neither to predict accurately nor to pick the preferred option. Rather the intention is to examine the implications of each scenario: how a user would fare within it, and the challenges for societies and communities.

Each of the scenarios set out above is plausible. Working with them, leaders might examine the strengths and implications of each. The question is: *who controls or influences what is to emerge?* How are the real interests of learners, our societies and the planet to be put first – above those of either vested interests or inertia?

In conclusion: Saving schools may help to save us

In thinking about the School of the Future we have noted that:

- Future-focused global organisations have collectively generated some powerful design principles
- Schools intentionally focused on becoming future-fit are combining these in different ways, related to context and ambition
- How they are combined has different implications for the use of time, space, people and technology – the basic elements of schooling; as well as choices around curriculum, pedagogy and assessment
- Visionary educators have in some instances created schools based on combinations of the design principles explicitly to address the fundamental challenges faced by societies – the *Archetypes* we explored in Chapter 1. They are undertaking the new job we need schools to do for us.

This last point is where we wish to end. A school of the future should not be imagined as, on the one hand, adjuncts of the powerful technologies humans are developing; nor even just as more human-centred relationally based organisations. We need to see them as a fundamental element in the range of new solutions humankind must evolve if we are to overcome and transcend the existential challenges that confront us. Schools have by no means outlived their usefulness: on the contrary. They are vital. They *need not* be analogue institutions in a digital age; but could be expressions of our determination to be truly, newly human.

A green revolution that saves our habitat and our existence upon it; a transformed approach to other species; genuinely democratic equitable societies; international cooperation; mental and physical health security – none of this is achievable unless we develop institutions that are explicitly aimed at contributing to these goals through the development of new humans. In short, it is about thriving at the global, societal, interpersonal and intrapersonal levels. Transformed schools are key to achieving this vision for our futures.

Notes

1 A number of organisations brought out COVID-related reflections whilst still at the height of the pandemic. See UNESCO op. cit. and OECD 2020(b).
2 Extract from interview featured on the Australian Learning Lecture website https://all-learning.org.au/.
3 See Carney, 2021 and Mazzucato, 2020.
4 On the skills of storytelling in public life, see Ganz, 2009.
5 www.big-change.org/pioneer-stories/new-zealand-education-conversation.
6 See www.education.govt.nz/news/the-future-of-education/.
7 For more detail, see www.education.govt.nz/our-work/changes-in-education/aotearoa-new-zealand-histories-in-our-national-curriculum/more-information-about-the-aotearoa-new-zealand-histories/#NZC.
8 Sinnema, Clare, and Stoll, L. Learning for and realising curriculum aspirations through schools as learning organisations, *European Journal of Education*, 55 (1): 9–23. 2020 https://onlinelibrary.wiley.com/doi/full/10.1111/ejed.12381?af=R.
9 Hannon, Valerie and Mackay, T. The Future of Educational Leadership: five signposts https://drive.google.com/file/d/1L82c_TMEDrQ2nx57Nw6fOCSZ4V9BMPIO/view?usp=sharing CSE, Melbourne, 2021.
10 Sanford K. and Hopper T., Educational Transformation: the BC Story, University of Victoria UVic Space, 2020 https://dspace.library.uvic.ca/handle/1828/12281.
11 Kaser, Linda, and Halbert, J., 2009.
12 See the Danish Rockwool Foundation www.rockwoolfonden.dk/en/projects/systeminnovation-hvad-kraever-det-at-forandre-et-system.
13 Leadbeater, Charles, and Winhall, J. *Building Better Systems: A Green Paper on System Innovation*. Rockwool Foundation, 2020.
14 See Breakspear, S., *Agile implementation for learning* CSE Seminar Series Paper 147, Centre for Strategic Education, Melbourne, 2016.
15 https://noiie.ca and www.educationalleaders.govt.nz/Pedagogy-and-assessment/Evidence-based-leadership/The-spiral-of-inquiry.
16 https://tll.gse.harvard.edu/design-thinking#:~:text=Design%20Thinking%20is%20a%20mindset,refining%20ideas%2C%20and%20testing%20solutions.
17 Interview with Valerie Hannon, 09/07/2020.
18 https://medium.com/future-of-school.
19 Luksha P., *Learning Ecosystems: an emerging praxis for the future of education*, 2020, retrieved from http://learningecosystems2020.globaledufutures.org.

92   *The leadership challenge of a generation*

20 https://hundred.org/en/innovations/whole-city-as-a-learning-environment#417e981d.
21 See also the *Ecosystems Learning Lab* that the World Innovation Summit (WISE) has set up: wise-qatar.org/ special-focus/designing-vibrant-and-purposeful-learning-comm unities.
22 www.csf.gov.sg/.
23 For example, the Welsh government offer a free futures-thinking toolkit for public servants www.futuregenerations.wales/wp-content/uploads/2020/02/PHW-Three-Horizons_FINAL.pdf; see also Shallowe et al., 2020.
24 OECD, 2020 op. cit.

References and further reading

Bell, W. *Foundations of Futures Studies: Human Science For a New Era*. London: Transaction Publishing, 2010.

Carney, M. *Value(s): Building a Better World for All*, New York: Harper Collins, 2021.

Ganz, M. *What is Public Narrative: Self, Us & Now, (Public Narrative Worksheet)*, Working Paper, Harvard, 2009. Available at nrs.harvard.edu/urn-3:HUL.InstRepos:30760283.

Halbert, J. and Kaser, L. *Spirals of Inquiry for Equity and Quality*, Canada: BC Principals and Vice-Principals Association, 2013.

Hannon, V., Thomas, L., Ward, S. and Beresford, T. *Local Learning Ecosystems: Emerging Models*, Toronto: WISE, 2018.

Kaser, Linda and Halbert, J. *Leadership Mindsets: Innovation and Learning In the Transformation of Schools*. Abingdon: Routledge, 2009.

Leadbeater, C. and Winhall, J. *Building Better Systems: A Green Paper on System Innovation*, Copenhagen: Rockwool Foundation, 2020.

Luksha, P., Spencer-Keyse, J. and Cubista, Joshua. *Learning Ecosystems: An Emerging Praxis for the Future of Education*, 2020. Accessed at learningeco systems2020.globa ledufutures.org.

Mazzucato, Marianna. *The Value of Everything: Making and Taking in the Global Economy*, New York: Hachette Book Group, 2020.

OECD. *Lessons for Education from COVID-19: A Policy Maker's Handbook for more resilient systems*. Paris: OECD, 2020(b).

Ransom, H. (2021) *The Leading Edge – Dream Big, Spark Change and Become the Leader the World Needs You to be*. Viking, 2021.

Scharmer, O (2013) *Leading from the Emerging Future: From Ego-System to Eco-System Economies*, New York: Penguin Random House.

Shallowe, Adanna, *et al. A Stitch in Time: Realising the Value of Futures and Foresight*. London: RSA, 2020.

Sharpe, Barry. *Three Horizons: The Patterning of Hope*. Bridport: Triarchy Press, 2013.

Smith, Scott. *How to Future: Leading and Sense-Making in an Age of Hyperchange*, London: Kogan Page, 2020.

Tetlock, P.E. *Superforecasting: The Art and Science of Prediction*. New York: Crown Publishing, 2016.

Appendix

Organisations reviewed

1.	Big Picture Learning	www.bigpicture.org/
2.	Carnegie Mellon Eberly Centre	www.cmu.edu/teaching/
3.	Chan Zuckerberg Initiative	https://chanzuckerberg.com/
4.	The Coalition of Essential School	http://essentialschools.org/
5.	Deans for Impact	https://deansforimpact.org/
6.	Education Reimagined	https://education-reimagined.org/
7.	Expeditionary Learning	https://eleducation.org/
8.	First Peoples Principles of Learning (Canada)	www.fnesc.ca/first-peoples-principles-of-learning/
9.	The High Tech High Group	www.hightechhigh.org/
10.	Institute of Applied Neuroscience	www.appliedneuro.org/about.html
11.	Knowledge Works	https://knowledgeworks.org/
12.	LEAP Innovations	https://leapinnovations.org/
13.	Learning Frontiers	www.innovationunit.org/wp-content/uploads/Issue-1-Learning-Frontiers-Insights-and-Ideas-FINAL.pdf
14.	Lego Foundation	www.legofoundation.com/en/
15.	New Pedagogies for Deep Learning	https://deep-learning.global/
16.	Next Gen Learning	www.nextgenlearning.org/
17.	OECD Innovative Learning Environments 7 Principles	www.oecd.org/education/the-oecd-handbook-for-innovative-learning-environments-9789264277274-en.htm
18.	OECD Education 2030 Learning Framework	www.oecd.org/education/2030-project/
19.	Remake Learning	https://remakelearning.org/
20.	Re-school Colorado	www.reschoolcolorado.org/
21.	Transcend Education	www.transcendeducation.org/
22.	XQ Institute	https://xqsuperschool.org/about/
23.	Yidan Prize	https://yidanprize.org/

Index

Page numbers in italics refer to figures.

3D printing 51
4.0 (US) 85
5 Minds for the Future (Gardner) 68
21st century skills 22

Academy for Global Citizenship, US 69
Acton Academy 79
adaptive expertise 48
advisory 60–61
Africa: Future Nation Schools 70; Spark Lynedoch 69
agile leadership 84
Agile Learning Centres 79
AI-driven learning programmes 5, 17, 50–51
Allen, Damian 86
anticipation 89
archetypes, for future: entrepreneurs and changemakers 72; environmental thriving 69–70; ethical leadership 70; human identity 72–73; newer landscapes of work 71–72; technological future 71; thriving 73–77
Ardern, Jacinda 81–82
Aristotle 17
Arnold, Matthew 22
arts education 36–38
Ashoka movement 72
augmented reality 51
Australia: Launceston Big Picture, Tasmania 49–50; Lumineer Academy, Melbourne 52–55; School of the Air 23; Swinburne University 86; Wooranna Park in Victoria 64, 71

Bali (Green School) 1–3, 59–60, 69
Barcelona (LearnLife) 6–7, 72, 84–85

Beare, Hedley 15
Beijing (Moonshot Academy) 72
Bentley, T. 23
Berger, Ron 62
Big Picture Learning 24, 93
biodiversity destruction 74
biotechnology 71
Black Lives Matter campaign 9
blockchain 71
Bosselman, John 47
Bourke, Ruby 1, 3, 59–60, 64, 65
bureaucrats 83

Cambodia (Liger Leadership Academy) 3–4, 56–57, 70
Canada: Farm Roots Mini School, British Columbia 65; First Peoples Principles of Learning 24, 28–29, 93
Carnegie Mellon Eberly Centre 24, 93
Carney, Mark 81
catalytic philanthropy 24
Centre for Research and Innovation (CERI) 27
Centre for Strategic Futures 87
CERI *see* Centre for Research and Innovation (CERI)
changemakers 72
Chan Zuckerberg Initiative 24, 93
child development 52
Christianity 22
Chung Nam Samsung Academy (CNSA) 50–51, 71
climate crisis 69, 74
climatic emergencies 11
CNSA *see* Chung Nam Samsung Academy (CNSA)
Coalition of Essential School 24, 93

Index

collaborative learning 60
commodification 81
community/societal thriving 75
computer-aided design 51
computer programming 52
COVID-19 pandemic xiv, 2, 11–13, 70, 73; challenges 86; futures thinking 13–16; opportunities during 12–13
Crosstown High School 42–45, 57
cultural transmission 22
Cummins, Paul 37
custodial function 22

D39C *see* Design39Campus (D39C)
Daisuke Suzuki 5
Dcon *see* Deep Learning Contest (Dcon)
Dean, Adrian 50
Deans for Impact 24, 93
deep learning 24, 48
Deep Learning Contest (Dcon) 5
democratic disappointment 18
Deschooling Society (Illych) 16
Design39Campus (D39C) 41–42
design principles xiv; changes 21–22; *Education and Skills 2030* 24, 27; First People's Principles of Learning 28–29; Innovative Learning Environments 26–27; Knowledge Works 25–26; learner experience 32–34, *33*, 56–67, *57*; newer 23; old functional model 22–23; operational philosophy 31, *32*, 46–55, *47*; synthesis and overview 29–30; values 30, *31*, 35–45, *35*
design thinking 33
digital technology 11, 16
direct instruction 33
disciplinary scholarship 22
diversity 40
Dweck, Carol 42

ecosystemic operations 31, 52–55
Education and Skills 2030 (OECD) 24, 26–28
education innovation 84
Education Reimagined 25, 26, 93
emotional intelligence 52
empathy 40
employment 71
empowerment 32, 63–67
enquiry spirals 84
entrepreneurs 72
environmental ignorance 70
environmental thriving 69–70
equity-focused values 30, 38–39

equity gap 12
ethical leadership 70
Eton College 70
expeditionary learning 24, 62, 93
experiential learning 47, 48
exploration enrichment programme 42
extended schooling 89

Farm Roots Mini School, British Columbia 65
Fenton, Sophie 52
Finland 86–87
First Nations' Education Steering Committee (FNESC) 29
First Peoples Principles of Learning (Canada) 24, 28–29, 93
flexible/dynamic operations 31, 49–50
Floyd, George 37
FNESC *see* First Nations' Education Steering Committee (FNESC)
forest schools 23, 69
formal learning 90
Fukuyama, Francis 73
future: literacy 87; possible/plausible/probable/preferred 14–15; proofing 89
Future Nation Schools Africa 70
Future of Learning 2030 Barometer exercise 86
Futures Literacy Laboratories (UNESCO) 14
futures thinking 13–16, 86–89

game-based learning 33
Gardner, Howard 68
Gates, Bill 14
Gordon, Sal 3
Gore, Al 2
Gorman, Amanda 36
Gorman, Gabrielle 36
Greece 22
green revolution 91
Green School Everywhere 2
Green School in Bali, Indonesia 1–3, 59–60, 69

Halbert, J. 83
Hammond, Linda Darling 62
Hardy, Cynthia 2
Hardy, John 2
Harri, Gwyn Ap 62, 79–80
Harris, Stephen 6–7
Harvard Study of Adult Development 75
hedge schools, Ireland 23
High Tech High Group 24, 93

96   *Index*

Holte, Jeff 4, 70
Hopper, T. 83
Hsu, Lillian 47–49
human-centred design 84
human identity 72–73
Hybrid High School, California 61
Hyman, Peter 39

ICP *see* Inclusive Campus Programme
    (ICP)
Identity (Fukuyama) 73
identity politics 73
identity promoting values 30, 39–41
Illych, Ivan 16
inclusion 32, 60–61
Inclusive Campus Programme (ICP)
    40–41
Inconvenient Truth, An (Gore) 2
India (Riverside School, Ahmedabad)
    40–41, 62, 64, 72
individualised learning 50
Industrial Revolution 22
informal learning 90
innovation 84–85
Innovative Learning Environments
    (OECD) 26–28
innovative providers 24
Institute of Applied Neuroscience 24, 93
integration 32, 59–60
integrative learning 3
Internet of Things (IoT) 71
interpersonal thriving 75
intrapersonal thriving 75
IoT *see* Internet of Things (IoT)
Ireland (Hedge schools) 23

Japan (Kosen Schools) 4–5, 71

Kaser, Linda 83
King's College, London 59
Kings School, Canterbury 22–23
KnowledgeWorks 25–26, 93
Kosen Schools, Japan 4–5, 71

Latitude High School, Oakland 47–49
Launceston Big Picture, Tasmania 49–50
leadership 12, 70; agenda 80–88; agile 84;
    cathedral thinking 78, 88; development
    41; focused schools 70; futures thinking
    86–89; for innovation 84–85; learning
    ecosystems 85–86; pandemic's gifts
    78–79; beyond pockets of brilliance
    79–80; professional debate 82–83;
    public will 80–82; *scenarios* frame

88–89; system leaders 83–84; *three-
    horizon thinking* frame 87–88
LEAP Innovations 24, 93
"learn-as-you-go" 90
learner agency (self-direction) 32, 63–67
learner experiences 32–33, 57; empower-
    ment 33, 63–67; inclusion 32, 60–61;
    integration 32, 59–60; personalisation 32,
    56–58; relationships 32, 61–63
learning: through AI 17, 50; collaborative
    60; deep 24, 48; ecosystems 85–86;
    expeditionary 24, 62, 93; experiential
    47, 48; focused operations 31, 46–49;
    formal/informal 90; game-based 33;
    integrative 3; nature-based 33; online
    17, 51; oracy 64; phenomenon-based
    33; plans 50; project-based 3–4, 33, 60;
    real 47, 52–55, 78–79; service 33
Learning Compass (OECD) 25
Learning Frontiers 24, 93
LearnLife, Barcelona 6–7, 72, 84–85
Lego Foundation 24, 93
liberal democracy 73
Liger Leadership Academy (LLA) 3–4,
    56–57, 70
Luksha, P. 85
Lumineer Academy, Melbourne 52–55

Mack, Aaliyah 38
Mandela, Nelson 39
Mary L. Booker Leadership Academy 70
material sciences 71
mental illness 75
Met Big Picture School (Rhode
    Island) 86
METERAI (AI-assisted system) 5
#MeToo movement 18
micro-schools 79
Miller, Riel 23
minorities 38
Moonshot Academy in Beijing 72
Muse School, California, US 69

nanotechnology 71
nature-based learning 33
New Pedagogies for Deep Learning
    24, 93
New Roads School, Santa Monica,
    California 36–38
New Zealand 8–9, 72, 81–82
Next Gen Learning 24, 26, 93
Nga Tapuwae, New Zealand 8–9, 72
noisy classrooms 39
Nova Pioneer School 70

NuVu, Cambridge, Massachusetts 60, 64–65, 72

OECD *see* Organisation for Economic Cooperation and Development (OECD)
online learning 17, 51
on-the-job training 4
open air schools 23
operations *32, 47*; ecosystemic 31, 52–55; flexible/dynamic 31, 49–50; learning focused 31, 47–49; technology enhanced 31, 50–51
oracy learning 64
Organisation for Economic Cooperation and Development (OECD) 15–16, 88; *Education and Skills 2030* 24, 26–28, 93; future school landscape 28; Innovative Learning Environments 24, 27, 93; plausibility for education 89–90
outsourced education 89

Papert, Seymour 21
passion projects 33
personalisation 26, 32, 56–58
phenomenon-based learning 33
Philosophy for Children (P4C) model 39
physicality 18
PISA *see* Programme for International Assessment (PISA)
planetary/global thriving 74
plausibility 14–15, 88
policy innovation 89
political will 81
Pommerening, Christopher 6, 84–85
prediction 14
problem solving 47
professional debates 82–83
professional development programmes 24
Programme for International Assessment (PISA) 27
project-based learning 3–4, 33, 60
prosumers 90
public will 79, 80–82
purpose-built schools 22
purpose driven values 30, 36–38

Quantum Camp 79

R&D (Research and Development) 84
racial inequality 38–39
real learning 47, 52–55, 78–79
Reimers, E. 16
relationships 32, 61–63

relevant values 31, 42–43
religions, fortifying 22
Remake Learning 24, 93
Re-school Colorado 24, 93
resource depletion 74
Rhode Island (Met Big Picture School) 86
Riverside in Ahmedabad, India 40–41, 62, 64, 72
Round Square 79
Roy, Arundhati 13
RSA/YouGov survey 13

Sanford, K. 83
scenarios frame 88–89
School 21, London 38–39, 62, 64
Schooling for Tomorrow project 27
School is Dead (Reimers) 16
School of the Air, Australia 23
school(s): about/for community 42; building thriving future 73; functions 17–18, 22–23; as learning hubs 89–90; low survival rate as institution 16–17; during pandemic 11–12; and real world learning 52–55; reconstructing 18–19; strikes 70
self-direction 32, 63–67
service learning 33
Sethi, Kiran Bir 40
Singapore 87
skills gaps 72
social action 36–38
social doctors 71
social-emotional skills 26
social mobility 22
South Korea (Chung Nam Samsung Academy) 50–51, 71
Spark Lynedoch, South Africa 69
Stirling, Arihia 8–9
strength-based values 30, 41–42
student agency 26
students, developing learning plans 50
Sustainable Development Goals (UN) 16
Swinburne University 86
system innovation 84
system leaders 83–84

Talent and Innovation Ecosystem 86
TCEC *see* Tri-County Early College (TCEC)
teamwork 52
technology 31, 50–51, 71
three-horizon thinking frame 87–88, *88*
Thrively (online programme) 41–42

98   *Index*

thriving future: of schools 73; in
    transforming world 74–77
Thunberg, Greta 78
Toshiki Tomihira 5
Transcend Education 24, 93
Tri-County Early College 5–6, 72, 86
trust 62

UNESCO 14, 18
United Kingdom (UK): Eton College 70;
    King's College, London 59; School 21,
    London 38–39, 62, 64; XP school in
    Doncaster 62
United States (US): 4.0 85; Crosstown
    High School, Tennessee 42–45, 57;
    Design39Campus, California 41–42;
    Hybrid High School, California 61;
    Latitude High School, Oakland 47–49;
    Muse School, California 69; New Roads
    School, Santa Monica, California 36–38;
    NuVu 60, 64–65, 72; Re-school
    Colorado 24, 93; Tri-County Early
    College 5–6, 72, 86

United World Colleges 70, 79
UN Sustainable Development Goals 16

values 30, *31, 35*; equity-focused 30,
    38–39; promoting identity 30, 39–41;
    purpose driven 30, 36–38; relevant 31,
    42–45; strength-based 30, 41–42
virtual reality 51

Ward, Joi 61
Whittle Schools and Studios 79
Williams, Luthern 37
Wooranna Park in Victoria, Australia
    64, 71
work, new landscape of 71–72
Wu, Susan 52

XP school in Doncaster 62
XQ Institute 24, 93

Yidan Prize 24, 93
youth unemployment 72

Printed in the United States
by Baker & Taylor Publisher Services